What Others Are Saying

Dr. James Taylor's book, *"It's Biblical, Not Political! How to Line Candidates Up Biblically"* is excellent! It is an insightful and powerful examination of the principles that made America the greatest nation in the world, and threats that challenge its very existence. Dr. James Taylor gives clear and profound answers to the nations' problems. I highly recommend every American read *"It's Biblical, Not Political! How to Line Candidates Up Biblically"*

—William Federer, President of
Amerisearch, Inc. and American Minute

"The Bible is timeless, ageless and limitless in its relevance. In a chaotic world full of political confusion and moral compromise, the Bible is the only constant on which we can truly build our foundation. Dr. James Taylor masterfully crafts an assertion that both fortifies doctrine and addresses critics."

—Randy Frerking, Enterprise Technical
Expert, Enterprise Platform Services

"A recent poll showed that 90% of pastors understood that the Bible speaks to all of the key public policy issues of the day, but fewer than 10% of pastors were actually teaching on those subjects. Into that void steps Pastor JT with exactly what the Church needs to learn before it can perform its assigned role to teach the nations."

—William J. Olson, Constitutional Lawyer and
former Reagan Administration Official

It's Biblical, Not Political! is an excellent guide for the Christian voter. Dr. Taylor does a masterful job of tying biblical history to modern day culture. Truly a must read!"

—Sharon Miner, Director of
Accountability for Sam Silverstein, Inc.

IT'S BIBLICAL, NOT POLITICAL!

DR. JAMES TAYLOR

IT'S BIBLICAL, NOT POLITICAL!

How to Line Candidates Up Biblically

TATE PUBLISHING
AND ENTERPRISES, LLC

Published by Tate Publishing & Enterprises, LLC
127 E. Trade Center Terrace | Mustang, Oklahoma 73064 USA
1.888.361.9473 | www.tatepublishing.com

Tate Publishing is committed to excellence in the publishing industry. The company reflects the philosophy established by the founders, based on Psalm 68:11,
"The Lord gave the word and great was the company of those who published it."

Book design copyright © 2015 by Tate Publishing, LLC. All rights reserved.
Cover design by Joshua Rafols
Interior design by Gram Telen

Published in the United States of America

ISBN: 978-1-68164-658-9
Religion / General
15.09.08

To my parents, Ronald and Shirley Taylor; sister, Sharon Miner; and late brothers, Al and Jack—whose example of Christ has made me who I am today.

Thank you for all you have done in my life. I love you.

Acknowledgments

I wish to acknowledge members of the Tate Publishing Company who encouraged me to continue to write this book after I became discouraged. I became discouraged at watching candidates say they are going to do one thing and then watch them do the opposite when they were voted into office. It was members of the Tate team who urged me to complete this work. Thank you.

Contents

Introduction

"I don't think a pastor should be involved in politics" are words I have heard many times. Oddly enough, I have only heard that statement from Christians. When a person says those words, they are revealing three things about themselves that I don't believe they know they are revealing.

First of all, they are revealing that they do not know much about American history. The American colonies were divided among religious denominations.

> Massachusetts was Puritan, Rhode Island was Baptist, Connecticut and New Hampshire were Congregationalist, New York was Dutch Reform, Delaware was Lutheran and Dutch Reformed, Pennsylvania was Quaker and Lutheran, New Jersey was Lutheran and Dutch Reform, Virginia was Anglican, Maryland was Catholic, North and South Carolina were Anglican and Georgia was Protestant. There was a great deal of intolerance among the different denominations. For example, Puritans were intolerant of Baptist, Congregationalist, and Quakers.

> The Anglican expelled the Puritans in Virginia and
> there was simply not much of a cooperative spirit
> amongst the colonies.[1]

It was due to the Great Awakening that preachers
began to cause the colonies to tolerate one another
and eventually unite. That would lead to the unity that
solidified the colonies to rebel against England. The Great
Awakening was characterized by incredible growth of
personal faith as well as a period of denominations crossing
denominational lines to work together as one. The pastors
of the Great Awakening began to concentrate on the areas
of the Scriptures on which almost all Christians agreed
rather than on the areas where there was disagreement.
They also preached practical Christianity, addressing daily
personal behaviors that had relevant applications to society.
They preached on moral issues such as integrity, courage,
drunkenness, profanity, and immorality. The sermons
addressed legislative policies of the day because they believe
that it was biblical, not political.

The pastors began to preach that we are all part of the body
of Christ, and in eternity, we are all going to be worshiping
God as one. In fact, when the Revolutionary War began,
the British came to the colonies (other British subjects)
and went after the preachers. A Christian nation (Great
Britain) goes to their fellow citizens, other Christians (the
thirteen colonies), and began to burn their churches. The
preachers wore black robes when they preached, and thus

they were called the Black Robed Regiment. The British believed that if they could get to the preachers, they could stop this rebellion in its cradle.

I recommend Dan Fisher's two-volume edition of *Bringing Back the Black Robed Regiment: A Call for Preachers Who Will Fight.* Dan Fisher is a patriot pastor, a representative for the state of Oklahoma, a godly man who loves his God, family, church, and country. For more information on the Black Robed Regiment, please get his books. Fisher details how the pastors made a difference in the shaping of America. He documents the role of the church and the preachers in calling the original thirteen colonies to unity, which ultimately led to the Declaration of Independence and the birth of the United States of America.

It was the preachers who rallied their congregations to become the famous minutemen who were ready on the spot to fight at a moment's notice. If not for the pastors of the Great Awakening, there would not have been a United States of America. The preachers were the backbone for the solidarity of the original thirteen colonies. The preachers united the colonies to take on the greatest military power in the world. The colonies had no army, navy, or even any power, but they had the intestinal fortitude to take on the most powerful force in the world. And we won…with the help of God.

At one point in American history, it was a requirement that all candidates for public office be a Christian. When the states were forming their constitutions, all thirteen made it a requirement. In the Delaware Constitution of 1776 (the other twelve state constitutions were similar), it states,

> Article 22. Every person who shall be chosen a member of either house, or appointed to any office or place of trust…shall…make and subscribe the following declaration, to wit: "I _____, do profess faith in God the Father, and in Jesus Christ His only Son, and in the Holy Ghost, one God, and blessed for evermore; and I do acknowledge the Holy Scriptures of the Old and New Testament to be given by divine inspiration."[2]

That is part of what one had to believe in order to hold public office in the United States of America. The Delaware Constitution went on to say that the candidate must acknowledge a belief in future rewards and punishment. He must believe that when he left office, he was to be accountable to God for what he did while he was in office. Boy…do we need a return to the philosophy of our Founding Fathers! I just used Delaware's Constitution as an example, but all thirteen colonies had similar statements. By the way, those statements are still in their constitutions today.

The second thing it tells me about them is that they are not familiar with the Bible. That is not unusual because for many Christians, they only open their Bibles on Sunday while they are in worship services. In fact, many don't take their Bibles at all because most churches use video projectors to project the Scriptures, which means that Christians do not bring their Bibles anymore to church. Matthew 28:18–20 reads

> And Jesus came up and spoke to them, saying, "All authority has been given to Me in heaven and on earth. "Go therefore and make disciples of all the nations, baptizing them in the name of the Father and the Son and the Holy Spirit, teaching them to observe all that I commanded you; and lo, I am with you always, even to the end of the age."[3]

The Bible commands us to take the message of Christ to the world. The Matthew statement is in the imperative mode, stating it is a command and not optional. I am required, as a child of God's, to proclaim the message of Jesus Christ in every avenue that I can. Being an example for Christ is not optional. I always tell people, "Unless God specifically tells you to stay, He has already commanded you to go."

The church has been sitting on the bench as an observer to the moral decay of America. Thirty years ago, if a pastor said from the pulpit, "Marriage is between one man and one woman," or "abortion is murder," the congregation would say, "Preach it, brother!" Today, they ask, "Pastor, why are you being political?" We, the church, have allowed topics the Bible clearly speaks on to become political issues. Issues such as same-sex marriage, global warming, illegal aliens, excessive debt, individual responsibility, respect for life, capital punishment, parental responsibility for raising children, national sovereignty, and many other issues are addressed in *It's Biblical, Not Political!* because God addressed them first. God addressed these issues before there was a United States of America. Today, many Christians think it is political and not biblical, just the opposite, and that is the problem. We, the body of Christ, do not know our Bible well enough to know what the Scriptures reveal about these biblical issues that we have allowed to become political issues.

Finally, the third thing it tells me about them is that they are unfamiliar with a dictionary. One of the definitions for *politics* is "to influence society" or "one's influence on society." So let me place this definition in the opening statement. The opening statement was "I don't think a pastor should be involved in politics." The amended statement now reads, "I don't believe a pastor should be involved with 'influencing society.'" What a statement for a Christian to make. If the pastor has no influence in society, how does the Great Commission get accomplished? How are people going to be taught about creation, global warming, marriage, morality, and the list goes on? In fact, we ask a politician, "What is your policy on abortion, same-sex marriage, global warming, immigration, or etc.?" What we are asking them is, "What is your influence on society on…?" You fill in the blank.

We say that so often and don't give it any thought about what we are asking.

I want you to hear the words of an evangelist in the late 1800s. The Rev. J. A. Garfield (1831–1881) said this:

> The people are responsible for the character of the Congress. If that body be ignorant, reckless, and corrupt, it is because the people tolerated ignorance, recklessness, and corruption. If it be intelligent, brave, and pure, it is because the people demand these high qualities to represent them in the national legislature. If the next centennial does not find us a great nation… It will be because those who represent the enterprise, the culture, and the morality of the nation do not aid in controlling the political forces.[4]

What a powerful statement! Our corruption in politics is because we, the church, tolerate and continue to vote for the same corruption to return to office. Did I mention that the Rev. James A. Garfield was also the twentieth president of the United States of America? President Garfield also preached revivals while he was in the White House as president. That should help answer the question, "Should a pastor be involved in politics?"

The answer to the question, "Should a pastor be involved in politics?" is a resounding *YES*! *It's Biblical, Not Political!* is designed to help the reader compare candidate's statements with how they line up with the Bible. It is the "in thing" for a candidate to claim that they are conservative. Somehow, they think that if they claim to be conservative, they will get more votes. What we have now is candidates clamoring to be more conservative than their challenger. *It's Biblical, Not Political!* will give you the firepower to ask the right biblical questions of any candidate. It also takes the Scriptures and organizes them in a way that makes it easy for any Christian to evaluate from a biblical perspective any candidate to see if that candidate lines up with the holy Scriptures.

Charles Finney, one of the great preachers of the 1800s, said this:

> If there is a decay of conscience, the pulpit is responsible for it. If the public press lacks moral discernment, the pulpit is responsible for it. If the church is degenerate and worldly, the pulpit is responsible for it. If the world loses its interest in Christianity, the pulpit is responsible for it. If Satan rules in our halls of legislation, the pulpit is responsible for it. If our politics become so corrupt that the very foundations of our government are ready to fall away, the pulpit is responsible for it....Politics are part of a religion in such a country as this and Christians must do their duty to the country as a part of their duty to God.... Christians seem to act as if they think God does not see what they do in politics. But I tell you He does see it, and He will bless or curse this nation, according to the course Christians take.[5]

I agree with Charles Finney that the problem is the pulpit. Pastors are so busy trying to keep their jobs that they do not do their jobs. It is the pastor's job to preach the Word of God boldly and not be fearful that someone might accuse them of being political. When I preach God's Word, I am not being political, I am being biblical. Christians are to make a difference in the world, and it is time to get off the bench and get into the game! It's biblical, not political!

One final point of clarification: you will discover that I write the same way I talk. I don't apologize for that because I want to keep it simple to understand and apply the message with ease.

1

America's Past and Present
A Generational Change

Jack Hibbs, pastor of Calvary Chapel in Chino Hills, California, summed up best the spiritual situation we face today in our nation: "It's a sad thing to watch a nation die on your watch."[1] America is caught up in a downward spiral of immorality and violence. We are reaping what we have sown since the 1960s when we turned our back on God and decided to do our own thing. In the process, the God who blessed us so richly has been shoved aside and treated with disdain as a nuisance.

We once honored God, but we have plunged into moral decay that has reached the point wherein the words of the prophet Jeremiah 6:15 reflect our nation: "They were not even ashamed at all; they did not even know how to blush." We have lost the ability to blush. Things that used to cause us embarrassment we now wear as a badge of honor. I was born in 1958, and the descent has happened rapidly. In the

'50s, things were different, and let us consider the following statements of truth:

- Abortionists were considered the scum of the earth and were sent to prison for the murder of children.

- Homosexuals were still in the closet, and it was considered deviant behavior by the medical professional community.

- Drugs were something you bought at a pharmacy (or "drug store").

- Alcoholism was considered a sin, not a disease.

- Public school students prayed in their classes, read the Bible, and creation was taught as an alternative to evolution.

- High school graduates could actually read their diplomas.

- The 10 Commandments were still legal.

- Houses and cars were never locked.

- Social security was a job, and living on welfare was considered a disgrace.[2]

Looking back over the last fifty years, I'm reminded of the old Virginia Slims cigarette television advertisement, which sums it up best: "We've come a long way, baby!" Yes, we have, and it has been all in the wrong direction. We are reaping what we have sown as we have systematically, over time, removed or diminished the impact of God in our country.

- Today, we spend more on gambling each year than we do on food.

- Today, we kill 4,000 babies a day in the name of "freedom of choice" for women.

- Today, our families are destroyed by an epidemic of spousal abuse, child abuse, and divorce.

- Today, we consume 55% of all the illegal drugs in the world, even though we constitute only 5% of the world's population.

- Today, our homes are fortresses with bars on the windows, guns in the cabinets, and electronic security systems monitoring the doors and windows.

- Today, our schools are filled with drugs, rebellion, and violence.

- Today, our governing bodies are full of corruption on all levels.

- Today, our churches are apathetic and compromised by worldliness.[3]

Our Founding Fathers believed that when they left office, they were to be accountable to God for what they did while they were in office. In fact, on the floor of the Constitutional Convention, they debated this very issue.

They asked themselves how God punishes a nation for sin. They knew how God punished individuals for their sin, but they went to the Scriptures to get an answer. George Mason (the father of the Bill of Rights) said on the convention floor: "As nations cannot be rewarded or punished in the next world, they must be in this. By an inevitable chain of causes and effects providence punishes national sins by national calamities."[4]

In his dialogue, Mason cited when Ahab and Jezebel were leaders of Israel and they were sinning, God sent Elijah the prophet to tell of the punishment. For three and a half years, it did not rain because of the national sin of the leaders. He tells of David when he numbered his troops. David was warned not to number his troops, but he did it anyway. God sent a plague upon Israel; it wiped out seventy thousand in Jerusalem. And it went on, all of which is contained in the Congressional Record. It was as if they were having a Sunday school class on the convention floor.[5] We could certainly use a Sunday school class on our congressional floor today.

I quoted Charles Finney in the introduction, one of the great preachers of the 1800s, he emphasized that the decay, moral lapse, degeneration, and worldliness in our world is squarely laid at the feet of the preachers. You cannot have a moral society without the guiding principles of Christianity. Finney also highlights that God is watching how we vote and what we support in politics.

> *If there is a decay of conscience, the pulpit is responsible for it. If the public press lacks moral discernment, the pulpit is responsible for it. If the church is degenerate and worldly, the pulpit is responsible for it. If the world loses its interest in Christianity, the pulpit is responsible for it. If Satan rules in our halls of legislation, the pulpit is responsible for it. If our politics become so corrupt that the very foundations of our government are ready to fall away, the pulpit is responsible for it....Politics are part of a religion in such a country as this and Christians must do their duty to the country as a part of their duty to God....Christians seem to act as if they think God does not see what they do in politics. But I tell you He does see it, and He will bless or curse this nation, according to the course Christians take.*[6]

It only took one generation for the children of Israel to go from God is God to Baal is God. When Joshua died, the Israelites did not train up their children in the Lord. As a result one generation later, God was no longer their God. We are in the days of Judges 21:25, "And everyone did what was right in his own eyes." We call it "Different strokes for different folks." Another popular statement is, "If it feels good, do it." With this type of mind-set, we have produced a whole generation as Judges 2:10 states, "Who did not know the Lord." We have a new generation that is growing up, and they do not know the Lord. They do not have a faith of their own. They hold on to their parents' coattails while they are going through their teen years, but when they get to college, they are leaving the church, and 75 percent of them are not coming back.[7]

Ben Franklin once said, "Whosoever shall introduce into public affairs the principles of Christianity will change the face of the world."[8] That is what happened in America. We founded the nation on biblical principles. It is important for us to take a stroll down memory lane to have perspective on America's heritage. America is the victim of revisionist historians who have change America's birth into a politically correct pile of mumbo jumbo.

Today, we hear a great deal about the separation of church and state, as if the church had nothing to do with the founding of this great union of ours. We are told that the Founding Fathers of our country were atheist and agnostics. That simply is not true. Fifty-two of the fifty-six Founding Fathers were Orthodox Christians. Examples of the Pennsylvania delegates are Benjamin Franklin (Deist), Robert Morris (Episcopalian), James Wilson (Episcopalian/Deist), Gouverneur Morris (Episcopalian), Thomas Fitzsimons (Roman Catholic), Thomas Mifflin (Quaker/Lutheran), George Clymer (Quaker/Episcopalian), and Jared Ingersoll (Presbyterian):

> With no more than five exceptions (and perhaps no more than three), they were orthodox members of one of the established Christian communions: approximately twenty-nine Anglicans, sixteen to eighteen Calvinists, two Methodists, two Lutherans,

two Roman Catholics, one lapsed Quaker and sometime Anglican, and one Deist, Dr. Franklin, who attended every kind of Christian worship, called for public prayer, and contributed to all denominations.[9]

Patrick Henry, who is famous for the statement, "Give me liberty or give me death," made a very interesting statement: "It cannot be emphasized to strongly or too often that this great nation was founded, not by religionist, but by Christians, not on religions but on the gospel of Jesus Christ! For this very reason people of other faiths have been afforded asylum, prosperity, and freedom of worship here."[10]

Almost all our Founding Fathers wrote tracts and pamphlets for the churches of their day. In fact, the executive board of the American Tract Society (out of Garland, Texas, who are still in existence today)[11] were all Founding Fathers of this country. The same men who wrote Bible school lessons are the same men who signed the Declaration of Independence. Some of the same men were on the boards of the American Bible Society, the Philadelphia Bible Society, and the Christian Constitutional Society.[12]

America's Educational System

When students first went to school, they were taught out of *The New England Primer*, the textbook of the American schools from 1690–1900. Since there was no such thing as separated classrooms, all the students learned together. *The Primer* would be the equivalent to a first grade reader. It started out teaching the alphabet and then putting words together. About a fourth of the way through, they begin to put phrases together for the students to memorize. *The Primer* would take a letter of the alphabet and put a phrase to it, for example:

A. A wise son makes a glad father, but a foolish son is the heaviness of his mother.

B. Better is a little with the fear of the Lord, than great treasure and trouble there with.

C. Come unto Christ all you that are heavy laden and He will give you rest.

D. Do not this abominable things that I hate sayeth the Lord.

E. Except a man be born again he cannot see the kingdom of God.[13]

Every one of the phrases attached to a letter came from the Bible. This is how our young people learned to read for three hundred years. In fact, the lessons in *The Primer* consisted of "Who is the first man? Who is the first woman? Who is the first murderer? Who is the first martyr? Who is the oldest man? Who built the ark? Who was the most patient man?"[14] and etc.

It sounds like a Sunday school lesson. *The Primer* was not a soft-shell look at the Scriptures; the questions were extensive as the child moved along in his education. With education like that, it is no wonder that at the age of fourteen, John Quincy Adams received a congressional diplomatic appointment to the Court of Catherine the Great in Russia. Adams said, "The highest glory of the American Revolution was this: it connected in one indissoluble bond the principles of civil government with the principles of Christianity."[15] He said the greatest achievement in the revolution was that our nation was going to use Christian principles to govern ourselves. That certainly does not sound like the words of an atheist, nor a person who wants to separate the church and the government.

John Jay, the first chief justice of the original Supreme Court and one of the three men most responsible for the Constitution, said, "Providence has given to our people the choice of their rulers, and it is the duty as well as the privilege and interest of our Christian nation to select and prefer Christians for their rulers."[16] That almost sounds absurd today. In the 1952 presidential campaign, one of the major issues was that Adlai Stevenson was a divorced man. Yet since that time, the White House has had some occupants that have, well…let's just say, lowered the integrity of the office of president by their moral lapses. When was the last time you heard someone say they were only going to vote for Christian leaders?

George Washington's Farewell Address, at one time, was noted as the most significant political speech given to the nation. After all, he had given forty-five years of his life in public service. After two terms in office, he said to America, this is what brought us to this point and what will keep us going: "Of all the dispositions and habits which lead to political prosperity, religion and morality are indispensable supports. In vain would that man claim the tribute of patriotism, who should labor to subvert these great pillars."[17]

We need to make sure we read the Founding Fathers in context. When they mentioned *religion*, that meant Christianity. It did not mean what it is today that engulfs all religions. That was not the case. In the Shakespearean classic *Romeo and Juliet*, Juliet asks the question, "Wherefore art thou, Romeo?" To the twenty-first-century reader, we interpret that to mean, "Where are you, Romeo?" But at the time Shakespeare wrote that phrase, it was a question of, Why did I fall in love with the relative of my family's archenemy? In our day, we read the word *religion* to mean all religions, and that simply was not the case back then. It meant Christianity.

Washington said we are where we are because of "religion [Christianity] and morality," and if we want to continue to be prosperous, we should keep them as our central focus. At one time, Washington's speech was in all the history books in its entirety. But fifty years ago, it was taken out. Is it no longer a significant speech? No, that is not the problem; the problem is what he said. Washington said that religion, meaning Christianity and morality, are essential pillars in order for our society to function properly. We are moving away from what he said will keep us going as a union.

Are we a moral nation today? Are we a Christian nation today? Pres. Barack Obama has proclaimed that America is no longer a Christian nation.[18] We are following in the footsteps of the children of Israel when it only takes one generation for a nation to move away from God. There is the old saying, "Those who cannot remember the past are condemned to repeat it." Not only are we not remembering the past, we are rewriting the past.

The most common form of government in the world is an oligarchy. An oligarchy is a country or business that is controlled by a small group of people. The Roman Empire went from a republic to a democracy to an oligarchy. We are following in their footsteps. In fact, if you ask people what kind of government we have, their response is, "Democracy." That answer includes elected officials who should know better. In the Pledge of Allegiance we say, "And to the *Republic* for which it stands." We are in stage two of the morphing into an oligarchy. It is important that we look at America's heritage.

America's Heritage

Have you ever wondered how it is that our nation has survived for so long? We have been very successful for the past 230-plus years. That is almost unheard of among contemporary nations. In that same 230 years, France has gone through fifteen completely different Constitutions. Russia has gone through four since 1918. Brazil has been through seven since 1822. Poland has gone through six since 1921. Afghanistan has had five since 1923. Italy is currently in its eighth form in the same time period. Yet we are still in our first. How has this nation lasted so long?

Political science professors at the University of Houston wanted to know the answer to that question. They began to collect all the writings of our forefathers. Their reasoning was that the writings would be able to tell them who the founders were quoting and getting their information from. They collected over fifteen thousand writings of the forefathers. They reduced it down to 3,154 that they felt had significant impact on the founding of America. It took them ten years to compile the information and find out who shaped the minds of our forefathers.

They found that the three most quoted men were Sir William Blackstone, Baron Charles de Montesquieu, and John Locke. However, four times more than they quoted Montesquieu, twelve times more than they quoted Blackstone, and sixteen times more than they quoted John Locke, they quoted the Bible. Thirty-four percent of all the quotes came directly from the Bible, and 60 percent were quoting men that used the Bible to arrive at their conclusions.[19]

Let me illustrate. Sir William Blackstone wrote *Commentaries on the Laws of England* in 1758. For 160 years, it was the law text of America. The Supreme Court quoted it regularly to define words, look at procedures, and settle law questions. Where did Blackstone get his information and ideas? He got them from the Bible. In fact, when he gave the law, he would give the Scripture reference from which it came.[20]

Many people have heard of Charles Finney. He was the Billy Graham of the 1800s. He was a revival evangelist who wanted to be a lawyer. He went to law school to become a lawyer, and while he was studying Blackstone, he became a Christian.[21] Let me repeat that. He went to law school to become a lawyer, and while he was studying Blackstone, he became a Christian. When was the last time a lawyer went to study law and learned about Jesus in the process? Ninety-four percent of what the forefathers quoted was based on the Bible, and 34 percent came directly from the Bible.

Even the way we set up our government came from the Bible. Have you ever wondered why we have three branches of government? Have you ever researched why we did something that no nation in the history of the world ever did? Our forefathers were very much interested in serving God and wanted that reflected in every aspect of

America's existence. The reason we have three branches of government is because of the book of Isaiah 33:22: "For the Lord is our judge, the Lord is our lawgiver, the Lord is our King; He will save us." Thus we have a judiciary branch to judge the laws, a legislative branch to make the laws, and an executive branch to enforce the law.

Not only did we get the concept of three branches of government from the Bible, they also put in the checks and balance and the separation of powers based on the writings of the prophet Jeremiah, particularly the entire seventeenth chapter.[22] The reason we still do not tax churches is because of the Scriptures: "We also inform you that it is not allowed to impose tax, tribute or toll on any of the priest, Levite's, singers, doorkeepers, Nethinim, or servants of this house of God" (Ezra 7:24).

Today, even our neighbors to the north (Canada) and to the south (Mexico) tax churches. When you examine the early records of Congress, it is amazing how many times delegates would get up and tell what they found in the Bible. The members of the house would respond with, "If it's in the Bible, then we want it in our government."[23] When was the last time a member of Congress got up and read from the Bible? The amazing thing is that they quoted the book of Deuteronomy the most.[24] That is certainly not the easiest book to read for personal quiet time. Yet our forefathers were using that on the floor of Congress as they were establishing our union.

In the Supreme Court case *The Church of the Holy Trinity v. United States*, in 1892, a group of people were trying to separate the teachings of Jesus from the government. The Church of the Holy Trinity had hired a minister from England, but he could not work because of previous laws passed in the United States. The church was trying to read the letter of the law to allow the pastor to enter America to be able to work. In order to accomplish this, they had to attempt to separate government from the teaching of Jesus. Justice Brewer, who delivered the opinion of the court, ruled:

> Our laws and our institutions must necessarily be based upon and embody the teachings of the Redeemer of mankind. It is impossible for it should be otherwise, and to this extent our civilization and our institutions are to be emphatically Christian.[25]

The case was only sixteen pages long, but they used eighty-seven historical precedents to prove their point. They quoted the Founding Fathers (eighteen different ones), the acts of the Founding Fathers, the acts of Congress, over sixty different historical precedents, and after eighty-seven, they said we could list more, but eighty-seven is enough to show that this nation is a Christian nation...and no legislative action can be taken against Christianity.[26] The court based their ruling partially on the precedents that are set. Usually, they will cite the precedents for their rulings.

That is significant to remember; we will come back to this later.

In 1844 a college in Philadelphia wanted to teach morality without talking about religion. The case was so unorthodox that it made it to the Supreme Court. The case dealt with the estate of Stephen Girard (seven million dollars), a native of France who came to America before the signing of the Declaration of Independence. He died and left his estate to the city of Philadelphia to build a college.

What caught the court's eye was the fact that Girard was a follower of the enlightenment philosophy popular in France. The philosophy was to keep God and government or Christianity and education apart. It also taught that morality could be attained apart from any religious principles. Girard did not want any church-related officer to be involved with the school whatsoever. The court said you will teach morality in *Vidal v. Girard*, 1844:

> The purest principles of morality are to be taught. Where are they found? Whoever searches for them must go to the source from which a Christian man derives his Faith the Bible. Why may not the Bible and especially the New Testament be read and taught as a divine revelation in the schools? Where can the purest principles of morality be learned so clearly or so perfectly as from the New Testament?[27]

The court ruled that you could not have a school that did not teach Christianity because that was the source of morality. That ruling is exactly the opposite of what is taking place today. We are told that we cannot teach morality in the school systems anymore. We call it by fancy names: value-free, morally neutral, values clarification, nondirective education, decision making education, process education, affective or experimental education, and even self-esteem building. No matter what we call it, the message is still the same. Isn't it interesting that at one time in American history it was not possible to separate Christianity from the classroom, yet today, every effort is made to make sure Christianity stays out of the classroom?

In *People v. Ruggles*, 1811, a very unbelievable ruling came down from the court. A man became angry and wrote a great deal of profanity. He would use what the Supreme Court called blasphemy. The texts of his remarks are recorded in the court documents. He said, "Jesus Christ was a bastard, and his mother must be a whore." He also made negative remarks about the Dalai Lama and Muhammad; however, the Supreme Court ruled that the Dalai Lama and Muhammad were imposters, and therefore, what he said about them was of no consequences. The court ruled, whatever strikes at the root of Christianity tends manifestly to the dissolution of civil government. If you attack Jesus Christ, you are attacking Christianity. If you attack Christianity, then you are attacking the foundation of the United States. Therefore, an attack on Jesus is an attack on the United States of America.[28]

The defendant was tried, found guilty, and was sentenced by the court to be imprisoned for three months and to pay a fine of $500. The court ruled an attack on Christ is literally an attack on the United States. Take note of the date of this case: 1811, thirteen years after the Constitution and the First Amendment was in place. We certainly have come a long way from our origin. Now we hear people screaming First Amendment and separation of church and state, despite the fact that those words do not appear in the Constitution or the First Amendment. The First Amendment reads,

> Congress shall make no law respecting an establishment of religion or inhibiting the free exercise thereof; or abridging the freedom of speech, or of the press; or the right of the people peaceably to assemble, and to petition the Government for a redress of grievances.[29]

Notice the words *church*, *separation*, nor *state* do not appear in the First Amendment. The Founding Fathers were very clear in their intentions. The First Amendment went through twelve editorial changes. The historical record leaves no doubt as to the intent of the framers:

> June 7 [1787]. Initial proposal of James Madison, "The Civil Rights of none shall be abridged on account of religious belief or worship, nor shall any national religion be established, nor shall the full and

equal rights of conscience be in any manner, nor on any pretext infringed."

July 28. House Select Committee. "No religion shall be established by law, nor shall the equal rights of conscience be infringed."

August 15. Full day of debate with many alterations and additions, with some question, still, whether any such amendment was necessary. Following the suggestion of his own state's ratifying convention, Samuel Livermore of New Hampshire proposed: "Congress shall make no laws touching religion, or infringing the rights of conscience."

August 20. Fisher Ames (Massachusetts) moved that the following language be adopted by the House, and it was agreed: "Congress shall make no law establishing religion, or to prevent the free exercise thereof, or to infringe the rights of conscience."[30]

The last version was sent to the Senate, which began its own work on the wording:

September 3. Several versions proposed in quick succession.

"Congress shall not make any law infringing the rights of conscience, or establishing any religious sect or society."

"Congress shall make no law establishing any particular denomination of religion in preference to

> another, or prohibiting the free exercise thereof, nor shall the rights of conscience be infringed."

> "Congress shall make no law establishing one religious society in preference to others, or to infringe on the rights of conscience."

> Passed at the end of the day: "Congress shall make no law establishing religion, or prohibiting the free exercise thereof."

> September 9. "Congress shall make no law establishing articles of faith or a mode of worship, or prohibiting the free exercise of religion."[31]

This version was sent back to the House where a conference committee convened to eliminate the differences in wording. This committee agreed that the final wording should be

> Congress shall make no law respecting an establishment of religion or inhibiting the free exercise thereof; or abridging the freedom of speech, or of the press; or the right of the people peaceably to assemble, and to petition the Government for a redress of grievances."[32]

It is clear that the Founding Fathers did not want what happened in Great Britain to happen in America. They did not want one denomination to rule the nation. That is the reason for the twelve editorial changes and for the final draft of the First Amendment. They were very clear that they wanted Christian principles in this nation and in the leadership of America, but they did not want one denomination to be the dominant denomination in America.

Separation of Church and State

Where did this idea of separation of church and state come from? In 1801 the Danbury Baptist Association of Danbury, Connecticut, heard a rumor that the Congregationalist denomination was about to be made the national denomination of America. As a result, they wrote a letter to President Thomas Jefferson. On January 1, 1802, Jefferson responded to the Danbury Baptist Association. In his remarks to the group, to address their fears, using the now-infamous phrase to assure them that the federal government would not establish them, nor any other denomination of Christianity, as the national denomination and that government would not regulate their religious expression:

> Believing with you that religion is a matter which lies solely between man and his God; that he owes account to none other for his faith or his worship; that the legislative powers of government reach actions only, and not opinions; I contemplate with sovereign reverence that act of the whole American people which declared that their legislature should "make no law respecting an establishment of religion,

or prohibiting the free exercise thereof," thus building a wall of separation between Church and State. Adhering to this expression of the supreme will of the nation in behalf of the rights of conscience, I shall see with sincere satisfaction the progress of those sentiments, which tend to restore to man all his natural rights, convinced he has no natural right in opposition to his social duties. I reciprocate your kind prayers for the protection and blessing of the common father and creator of, and tender you, for yourselves and your religious Association, assurance of my high respect and esteem.[33]

The separation phrase was a very common-used colloquialism of that day. Jefferson was using this phrase to encourage the Danbury Baptist Association to understand that the government would protect them rather than interfere with their religious beliefs and expressions. In referring to this phrase, James Adams said,

Jefferson's reference to a "wall of separation between Church and State"...was not formulating a secular principle to banish religion from the public arena. Rather, he was trying to keep government from darkening the doors of church.[34]

In 1853 Congress was petitioned by a group that wanted to separate the church and the state. The case was referred to a house committee to investigate the possibilities of separating the government from the church. It took them one year to investigate to see if it was possible to separate the two entities. At the end of that year, they gave a report to both houses. On March 27, 1854, Mr. Meacham, speaking for the House Judiciary Committee, gave their report (the Senate's was virtually the same):

> Had the people, during the Revolution, had a suspicion of any attempt to war against Christianity, that Revolution would have been strangled in its cradle. At the time of the adoption of the Constitution and the Amendments, the universal sentiment was that Christianity should be encouraged, but not only one sect. Any attempt to level and discard all religion would have been viewed with universal indignation.... In this age there is no substitute for Christianity.... That was the religion of the Founders of our Republic; and they expected it to remain the religion of their descendants!... The great vital conservative element in our government is the belief of our people in the pure doctrine and the divine truth of the gospel of Jesus Christ.[35]

Those wanting to separate God from government found no allies in either the courts or the Congress. In 1878, in a case called *Reynolds v. United States*, the Supreme Court pulled Jefferson's speech and quoted it in its entirety. This case involved the Mormon Church claiming the First Amendment to practice polygamy. Using Jefferson's address, the court affirmed that the purpose of separation was to protect rather than limit public religious expression.[36] The United States Supreme Court ruled,

> It (Jefferson's letter) may be accepted almost as an authoritative declaration of the scope and effect of the Amendment thus secured. Congress was deprived of all legislative power over mere (religious) opinions, but was left free to reach actions which were in violation of social duties or subversive of good order.[37]

The Supreme Court went on to define what they meant:

> The rightful purposes of civil government are for its officers to interfere when principles break out into overt acts against peace and good order. In this... is found the true distinction between what properly belongs to the Church and what to the State. [38]

That while the government was not free to interfere with opinions on religion, which is what frequently distinguished denominations from one another, it was still responsible to enforce civil laws according to Christian standards. In other words, separation of church and state pertained to denominations, not to Christian principles. Therefore, on that basis, the court ruled that the Mormon practice of polygamy and bigamy was a violation of the Constitution because it was a violation of basic Christian principles. The court said that Jefferson's wall existed to protect the church from the government but also said Christian principles are not to be separated from government.[39]

But nearly seventy years after the Reynolds case, in 1947 the court used only eight words of Jefferson's letter in a case called *Everson v. The Board of Education*: "The First Amendment has erected a wall between church and state. That wall must be kept high and impregnable. We could not approve the slightest breach."[40] This was the first time there was a reversal. Plus they cited no precedents nor previous cases, none. The Supreme Court pulled part of Jefferson's speech and just made the statement. When something is ruled unconstitutional, that meant that the forefathers would not have wanted that to occur in America. Yet it is very clear that our forefathers wanted very much for Christianity to play a dominant role in the shaping of our country. This reversal came out of the clear blue. Dr. William James was opposed to church and government being merged together. He is also known as the father of modern psychology. He said, "There is nothing so absurd but if you repeat it often enough people will believe it."[41]

In a 1958 case, *Bear v. Kolmorgen*, one of the justices wrote in his remarks:

> Much has been written in recent years concerning Thomas Jefferson's reference in 1802 to "a wall of separation between church and state."... Jefferson's figure of speech has received so much attention that one would almost think at times that it is to be found somewhere in our Constitution.[42]

As a note of interest, while the phrase "separation of church and state" is not found in the United States Constitution, Declaration of Independence, or Bill of Rights, it is found in another prominent document. The constitution of the former Soviet Union reads, "Article 124: In order to ensure to citizen's freedom of conscience, the church in the U.S.S.R. is separated from the State, and the school from the church."[43]

It seems that, because of the current court's rulings, we have more similarities with the former Soviet Union than we might have thought; although they seem to have more religious practice in schools under their constitution than we do under ours. Tim LaHaye, in his book *Faith of Our Founding Fathers*, records a sad irony to this issue:

> Who would have believed that the Supreme Court in 1980 would uphold the decision of a Kentucky school board (in Stone vs. Gramm) that the Ten Commandments, the basis of English law and the most important code of laws ever written, were illegal to display on the walls of the public schools because they represented a religious symbol? Ironically, just a few weeks before the Court's decision, some Polish high school students had demonstrated openly against their countries communist authorities for ordering the removal of the Catholic crucifix that still adorned the walls of their public schools and the government backed down. Americans cheered the courage of those young people for speaking out against their repressive

government. Yet when our atheistically dominated Supreme Court removed the Ten Commandments from our halls, not a whimper was heard."[44]

The Removal of Bible Reading and Prayer in the Public Schools

In a series of court cases, *Engel v. Vitale*, 1962 (which banned state-authored prayer in public schools); *Murray v. Curlett*, 1963 (which banned the mandatory prayer recital in public schools); and *Abington v. Schempp*, 1963 (which banned the Lord's Prayer and Bible reading in public schools) prayer and religious instruction were removed from our public schools in 1962 and 1963. In the June 25, 1962, *Engle v. Vitale* case, this was the first time the Supreme Court separated Christian principles from public education. As a result, school prayer was removed. The *World Book Encyclopedia*, 1963 edition, stated that this was a new doctrine. In this case, they cited no precedents, used no legal cases or historical incidents. Remember, in *The Church of the Holy Trinity v. United States*, the court cited eighty-seven precedents to support their ruling, what a change. With the other two cases mentioned above, by the end of 1963, prayer and Bible reading were effectively removed from the public education system.

What happened to make this change, where did America decide to change course from the founders of the constitution? On June 17, 1963, in the *Abington v. Schempp* case, they effectively removed Bible reading from the public schools of America. The court's reasoning, "If portions of the New Testament were read without explanation, they could be, and had been psychologically harmful to the child."[45]

This again was a new statement. How did we get to this point? Franklin said, "Whosoever shall introduce into public affairs the principles of Christianity will change the face of the world."[46] The Supreme Court stated, in the *Vidal v. Girard* case where a Philadelphia school wanted to separate morality from religion, "Why may not the Bible and especially the New Testament be read and taught as a divine revelation in the schools? Where can the purest principles of morality be learned so clearly or so perfectly as from the New Testament."[47] Now we are told if children read the New Testament, it is psychologically harmful to children.

The 1962, *Engel v. Vitale* case, which declared public school prayers as unconstitutional, was over this prayer: "Almighty God we acknowledge our dependence on Thee, and we beg Thy blessings upon us, our parents, our teachers, and our country."[48] That prayer only acknowledged God and did not contain the word *Jesus* at all. Eight years later, when the Supreme Court was referring back to this case, they said that prayer was a "to whom it may concern prayer." In other words, "If there is somebody up there, and you happen to be listening, we're praying." Yet that prayer was ruled unconstitutional for mentioning the name of God once. The Declaration of Independence mentions God four times. Does that mean that the Declaration of Independence is unconstitutional because it mentions God four times? Does that mean that our money is unconstitutional because we print on our currency "In God we trust"?

In 1963, the Supreme Court did a survey before they ruled on the *Engel v. Vitale* case and included the survey in their ruling. They found that only three percent of the American public profess no belief in religion, and 97 percent believed in God.[49] This was the first time that the court sided with the minority. This was the precedence for the minority to rule. From this case, three percent were going to decide how the other 97 percent were to conduct themselves.

George Washington, in his Farewell Address, made the following statement: "Reason and experience both forbid us to expect that national morality can prevail in exclusion of religious (Christian) principles."[50] Even Washington recognized that apart from Christianity, our nation's morality is in jeopardy. We are moving in a direction to take the principles of Christianity completely out of our lives as a nation. Consider the 1980 case of *Stone v. Gramm* out of Kentucky. A school had copies of the Ten Commandments hanging on the walls. It would be the equivalent of hanging a picture of George Washington or Abraham Lincoln on the wall. The court ruled that it was "passive display" by having the Ten Commandments on the wall and stated,

> If the posted copies of the Ten Commandments are to have an effect at all, it would be to induce the school children to read them, meditate upon them, perhaps, to venerate and obey the commandments, this is not a permissible objective.[51]

The Supreme Court ruled that hanging a copy of the Ten Commandments in the classrooms was unconstitutional because students might read them and practice them. Here are the Ten Commandments:

1. You shall worship only God and have no other God before me.

2. You shall not make a graven image or idol to worship.

3. You shall not take the name of the Lord your God in vain, for the Lord will not leave him unpunished who takes His name in vain.

4. Remember the Sabbath day, to keep it holy.

5. Honor your father and mother that your days may be prolonged in the land which the Lord your God gives you.

6. You shall not murder.

7. You shall not commit adultery.

8. You shall not steal.

9. You shall not bear false witness against your neighbor.

10. You shall not covet…the things that belongs to your neighbor.[52]

Do you realize that had the Ten Commandments came from Aristotle, Plato, or someone else they would still be allowed to hang in our schools? But because they came from the Bible, you can't read them. Is this what our Founding Fathers wanted? Did they want our children to not know the Ten Commandments? The court was concerned that our children might read the Commandments and practice them. The court ruled it was unconstitutional for students to read "don't murder," "don't steal," "don't commit adultery," "don't lie," "honor your parents," and etc. No wonder we have so many problems with drive-by shootings, thievery, promiscuity, people not telling the truth, and kids being disrespectful to their parents and those in authority.

Before God was removed from schools, polls among educators listed the top offences in the public schools (1960): (1) talking, (2) chewing gum, (3) making noise, (4) running in the halls, (5) getting out of turn in line, (6) wearing improper clothing, and (7) not putting paper in the wastebasket. When was the last time you heard a teacher say, "I'm going to quit! I can't take it anymore, those children never put paper in the waste basket"? In a *USA Today* poll in September 1985, the list has changed drastically: (1)

rape, (2) robbery, (3) assault, (4) burglary, (5) arson, (6) bombings, (7) murder, (8) suicide, (9) absenteeism, (10) vandalism, (11) extortion, (12) drug abuse, (13) alcohol abuse, (14) gang warfare, (15) pregnancies, (16) abortions, and (17) venereal disease.[53] We have come a long way, and it is all in the wrong direction.

James Madison, the chief architect of the constitution, stated,

> We have staked the whole future of American civilization, not upon the power of government, far from it. We have staked the future of all our political institutions...upon the capacity, of each and all of us, to govern ourselves, to control ourselves, to sustain ourselves according to the Ten Commandments of God.[54]

And yet, in 1980, the Supreme Court ruled that the Ten Commandments are unconstitutional. We have deviated from our Fore Fathers' design for this great union. Thomas Jefferson made the statement: "The reason Christianity is the best form of government is that Christianity is the only form of religion in the world that deals with the heart."[55]

In the Old Testament, Ten Commandments, it says, "You shall not commit murder." But Jesus dealt with the heart: "You have heard that the ancients were told, 'You shall not commit murder,' and 'Whoever commits murder shall be liable to the court.' But I say to you, everyone who is angry with his brother shall be guilty before the court."[56]

In the Old Testament, Ten Commandments, it says, "You shall not commit adultery." But Jesus dealt with the heart: "You have heard that it was said, 'You shall not commit adultery;' But I say to you, that everyone who looks on a woman to lust for her has committed adultery in his heart.'"[57] Jesus felt that if you take care of the hatred, you will not commit the murder. He felt if you take care of the lust, you will not commit the adultery. Christianity, as Thomas Jefferson suggested, is the only world religion that deals with the heart. That is why Jefferson felt as he did. If our hearts are right, the rest of the government will fall into place. John Adams, the second president of the United States of America, stated,

> "We have no government armed with power capable of contending with human passions unbridled by morality and religion….Our Constitution was made only for a moral and religious people. It is wholly inadequate to the government of any other."[58]

Abraham Lincoln was asked during the Civil War, "Do you think God is on our side in this civil war?" Lincoln's response, "I am not at all concerned about that, for I know that the Lord is always on the side of right. But it is my constant anxiety and prayer that I and this nation should be on the Lord's side."[59]

Roger Sherman holds a unique and distinguishable position among the Founding Fathers. He is the only one who signed the nation's four major documents: the Articles of Association of 1774, the Declaration of Independence in 1776, the Articles of Confederation in 1777, and the Constitution in 1787. At the convention, he proposed the compromise between the larger and the smaller states whereby one house of Congress would have representation based on population, and the other house would have equal votes between states, our current systems. He believed strongly that Christianity and the Bible were to be a part of government policy.

While in Congress, he objected to a War Committee report that recommended five hundred lashes as a punishment to be imposed by court-martials. Sherman successfully argued that Deuteronomy 25:3 limits the number of lashes to forty: "Forty stripes he may give him, and not exceed: lest, if he should exceed, and beat him above these with many stripes, then thy brother should seem vile unto thee."[60]

In 1776, when serving on a congressional committee, which wrote instructions for an embassy going to Canada, Sherman included an order that the delegation was "Further to declare that we hold sacred the rights of conscience, and may promise to the whole people, solemnly in our name, the free and undisturbed exercise of their religion" but added that all civil rights and right to hold office were to be extended to persons of any Christian denomination.[61]

This is yet another example of a Founding Father with strong opinions about basing government and public policy on Christianity. Our framers made powerful statements about Christianity and the necessity for it to remain a part of government. Charles Finney, after his conversion to Christianity while attending law school, made a strong statement about politics in America.

> The Church must take right ground in regards to politics. Politics are part of a religion in a country as this, and Christians must do their duty to the country as part of their duty to God. He will bless or curse this nation according to the course that Christians take in politics.[62]

I could go on and on about our heritage as a Christian nation, but this gives you the general idea. We have come a long way from where we started, but it's all in the wrong direction. I would strongly encourage the reader to engage in further study from the reference materials. It is not my intention, in these few pages, to contain all the documented proof of our heritage. This is just a small attempt to give you a baseline of our Godly heritage.

I believe we are now at the point of 2 Timothy 3:1–5:

> But realize this, that in the last days difficult times will come. For men will be *lovers of self, lovers of money,* boastful, arrogant, revilers, disobedient to parents, ungrateful, unholy, unloving, irreconcilable, malicious gossips, without self-control, brutal, haters of good, treacherous, reckless, conceited, *lovers of pleasure* rather

> than lovers of God, holding to a form of godliness,
> although they have denied its power; Avoid such men
> as these.[63] (Italics mine)

Notice that this prophecy predicts that this society will love three things: self, money, and pleasure. The love of self is humanism; this is the religion of America today. The love of money is materialism; that is America's God. When your religion is focused on self, and your god is money, the result is always a lifestyle based on the love of pleasure, which is hedonism. Needless to say, that is the lifestyle of America. "If it feels good, do it" is our national motto. Now, stay with me, when your religion is humanism, and your god is money, and your lifestyle is the pursuit of pleasure, then the payoff is nihilism, which is despair. When you read the 2 Timothy passage, the Apostle Paul is describing despair. We have moved away from the biblically sound teachings of God's Word as a union.

We have moved so far away from the founders that I believe we are under the judgment of God. We are under the wrath of God! I am first and foremost loyal to Jesus Christ, not to a political party. Whenever a Christian is more loyal to his political party than he is to his Savior, that Christian has a problem. When I go to the grocery store, I am still a Christian. When I go to an athletic event, I am still a Christian. When I step into the voting booth, I am still a Christian. I vote based upon issues. I look at economic issues, social issues, and foreign affairs issues to discern the biblical orientation of any candidate or politician.

The reason our country is in such a mess is because Christians have allowed our union to be in this mess. We are complacent, in fact, many of the following issues many Christians do not know that the Bible speaks on them. When I speak on this subject, the most common comment I receive is, "I didn't know the Bible said that?" What is sad is when I hear that statement from the pastors. With all due respect to my Christian brethren, you have access to the same Bible that I do. How is it that you cannot understand the clarity of God's Word? Jesus came to set us free from bondage. He says in John 8:32, "And you will know the truth, and the truth will make you free."[64] Please note that it is the truth that you know that sets you free.

2

God's Word Is the Standard of Truth

The Importance of Truth

God's Word is the standard of truth, John 17:17 says, "Sanctify them in the truth; Your word is truth." Please notice that verse ends in a period. That means it does not say God's Word is truth plus my opinion, God's Word is truth plus my experience, God's Word is truth plus what my pastor told me, or God's Word is truth plus anything else you place next to it. We must pass everything through the grid of God's Word to see if it can pass through, for that is the truth test. Since God's Word is the truth, it becomes the standard. We as Christians are responsible to be obedient to God's Word and not pick and choose which passages we will follow and which ones we will not follow. It is the responsibility of the pastor to boldly share the Word of God with his or her flock.

In the movie *A Few Good Men*, those of you who are familiar with the film, you will recall that as the film comes to an end, there is an explosive scene in it when the young lawyer, Tom Cruise, is face-to-face with Jack Nicholson, the commander in charge. He is confronting him on the accuracy of his testimony in the final courtroom scene. Tom Cruise confronts the general and stares into his eyes and says, "Sir, I want the truth!" And in a way that only Jack Nicholson could respond, he looked back at the young lawyer and said, "Truth, you can't handle the truth!"

I want to point out there is such a thing as truth. The Hebrew word for *truth* is the word that meant "firmness." It means that there was a solid body of facts that a person could rest on known as truth. In the New Testament, it came to be known as openness. This became known as the idea that there was a way that you can open up reality and see things as they really are. It is called truth, $1 + 1 = 2$. If you are from China, $1 + 1 = 2$, if you are an American, $1 + 1 = 2$; no matter where you are in the world, there is a body of mathematical truth. What is true of math is true of life. There is a body of facts that governs us; God calls that truth.

The question you and I face is not if there is truth, but where do we go to find truth. "And we know that the Son of God has come, and has given us understanding, so that we may know Him who is true, and we are in Him who is true, in His son Jesus Christ. This is the true God and eternal life" (1 John 5:20).

In order to view something as true, it must find its roots in God. Truth can only be measured as truth against a truth standard. If you do not have a standard of truth, you never know if something is true. The reason why we don't believe some of the people who tell us things is because they have questionable character, or we don't know them real well to believe what they say.

The reason why there is truth is because there is a God. God is truth. You and I don't have to guess about right or wrong, good and bad because there is a body of truth. And that body of truth is rooted in the only true God. God tells the truth about life, death, heaven, hell, money, child-rearing, marriage, sex, and many other things. He tells the truth about everything; therefore, when you find God, you have found truth. God says truth is real.

"Only God is true" (John 17:3). "You shall know the truth and the truth shall set you free" (John 8:32). "God reveals truth…thy word is truth" (John 17:17). There is such a thing as truth. We as Christians don't have to wallow in a sea of relativity. Relativity means what is true today is not true tomorrow. Relativity means it's true because I like it, or I want it, or I feel it. The reason why we as Christians can take our stand is because we have truth in a world that doesn't want truth. There are benefits of knowing and living by the truth.

The first benefit is knowing the truth allows the believer to experience grace, mercy, and peace. "Grace, Mercy and peace will be with us, from God the father and from Jesus Christ, the son of the father, in truth and love" (2 John

1:3). Many of us are looking for more grace from God, mercy from God, or more peace from God. And we wonder why we don't have more peace or more mercy or pity and while we're not experiencing more grace. The question then becomes, are you living in the truth?

Grace, mercy, and peace only come in connection with the truth. God never gives you His blessing when you are going to contaminate His truth. If you play games with the truth, you play with the goodness of God experienced in your life. If you want the peace of God, you have to be under the truth of God. If you want the mercy of God, you have to be under the truth of God. If you want the grace of God, you have to tell the truth. That's why the Bible says there is no forgiveness of sin until you're willing to confess the truth.

"If you confess your sins He's faithful and just to forgive us of our sins and cleanse us from all unrighteousness" (1 John 1:9). The word *confess* means "to agree with." He wants to know if you will call sin what it is. He doesn't want to hear about a mistake, a bad habit, or everybody does it. He wants the truth. How do I know it is the truth? Because He is the truth, and He calls it sin. Since God calls it sin, don't you give it any other name. Unlike us and Jack Nicholson's character, God can handle the truth. So if you want God giving you what you don't deserve, if you want Him to feel your pain and hurt and feel what you are going through, mercy, or if you want Him to calm your inner spirit, you must be willing to allow Him to confront you and me with the truth. And the truth is taken from the Scriptures.

Secondly, knowing the truth keeps you from being deceived. "For many deceivers have gone out into the world (not a few a bunch of them). Those who do not acknowledge Jesus Christ as coming in the flesh. This is the deceiver and the anti-Christ" (2 John 1:7). Did you read that? There are a bunch of deceivers out there, tricksters, informational magicians. We all like a good magic show. It's amazing how they can create an illusion of the truth. With sleight of hand, they have the ability to make it appear that people are sawn in half and disappear out of thin air. You stand back and say wow, how did he do that? He tricked you! He makes things appear one way when actually, they were another way. John says there are many deceivers that are out in this world tricking people regarding the truth. They can dupe people into believing it is the truth.

How do you measure the truth? "For many deceivers have gone out into the world those who do not acknowledge Jesus Christ as coming in the flesh." The way you measure the truth is not by how well people speak. It is not by what books they read. It is what they know and say about Jesus Christ. He is the Son of God unlike anyone else. It doesn't matter how many people you can gather at an auditorium, how many social programs you have, how many economic initiative you have. All of those are legitimate and have their place, but people are being deceived. Jesus Christ stands in a class by Himself. He is not to be compared with anyone else, and to do so is to diminish the Eternal Son of God. So we need to be clear on this matter because too many Christians are being duped. It's not just that they're legitimizing social programs, they are buying into a wrong God. It frees you from being deceived when you know the truth.

Thirdly, knowing the truth keeps you from losing your reward. "Watch yourself, that you do not lose what we have accomplished, but that you may receive a full reward" (2 John 1:8). When you defect from the truth, you lose your reward. God has rewards for believers. None of us get all of our rewards on earth. Many of the good things that you have done that deserve a pat on the back you won't get here. I've learned a long time ago to stop looking for pats on the back on earth because you don't get them as you may deserve them. But God is a great record keeper. And God knows of our work and faithfulness. But he says if you mess with the truth, that will cause you to lose your reward. Notice he says, "Make sure you receive a full reward," which means you must watch yourself and don't be tricked and duped. You are to measure your life by the measuring rod of Jesus Christ. He should be the standard: going back to his previous point, "Jesus has come in the flesh." That means God has become man in the person of Jesus Christ.

He says don't lose your reward. He says have a passion for truth. My passion is that God's people may never leave the truth. Paul (Acts 20:25–38) told the elders at Mellitus that there are going to be many deceivers who are wolves dressed in sheep's clothing. "Be on guard for yourselves and for all the flock, among which the Holy Spirit has made you overseers, to shepherd the church of God which He purchased with His own blood. I know that after my departure savage wolves will come in among you, not sparing the flock; and from among your own selves men will arise, speaking perverse things, to draw away the disciples after them" (Acts 20:28–30). He says be on guard. Because if you defect from the truth, which is the revelation from God through His son Jesus Christ, you lose your rewards.

The fourth thing he says, knowing the truth is essential for maintaining fellowship with God. "Anyone who goes too far and does not abide in the teaching of Christ, does not have God, the one who abides in the teaching, he has both the Father and the Son" (2 John 1:9). The word *abide* is John's word for intimacy. The Greek word *abide* means "to stay" or "to remain." The concept of abiding means to stay in close proximity. You can't be close to Christ without being close to His teaching.

Christ is not just a feeling in your gut. It is dependent on information about Christ before you can feel good in Christ. Intimacy with God is closely aligned with abiding in His word. Abiding is closely aligned with staying in touch with Him. That is drawing from Christ and His word to have an intimate relationship with Him. If you leave the truth, you leave the fellowship. And many of us are no longer close to Christ because we are tampering with everything else outside of the truth. We pick up our newspaper to see how our horoscope reads. That is tampering with the truth. God says the heart of idolatry is looking at the creation to tell you what should only be told to you by the Creator. We fool around with things that are outside of the truth and are not part of what God has revealed as part of the teachings of Christ recorded in His word. And we wonder why he seems so far away, because you are not abiding in the teachings of Christ. We're letting everything else tell us what we are to believe and what to think.

Sixthly, knowing the truth is the standard by which you measure the successful Christian life. "For I was very glad when brethren came and bore witness to your truth, that is, how you are walking in truth. I have no greater joy than this, to hear of my children walking in the truth" (3 John 1:3–4). How do you measure the success of your Christian life? There is a measuring rod for your spiritual life, and that is the standard of God's Word. Too many Christians are living their lives, saying, I think this and I feel that. Well, my opinion is, we are not here for your opinion. God did not ask you to read this book to tell you what I think. This is not an advice club. God has a standard, and I am held to that standard. You are held to that standard, and that standard is the truth. It is a body of facts that governs us. It is the truth, and we are to apply and walk in truth. It is a way of life.

Next, knowing the truth allows you to share in the blessings of others. "Therefore we ought to support such men, that we may be fellow workers with the truth" (3 John 1:8). When you support those who give the truth, you get credited with their blessing. The word is *fellow workers*. When you open up your heart and your home to people, when you open your resources for ministry, you get the blessing of their ministry. I give as much as I possibly can, not only to my church, where most of my giving goes, but to other ministries around the world, because at the judgment seat of Christ, I don't only want credit for my church; I want all the credit I can get attached to my account.

The question of any ministry is to ask, are they faithful to the truth? Are they faithful to God's Word? Are they consistent in their testimony? God credits your account with the blessing that He gives them because you shared in their commitment to the truth. And when they took the true word out, because we were fellow workers in the truth, because we were supporters of them taking the word, credit comes back to our account. So he says your Christian life is blessed because you have been used of God as a fellow worker with others.

The Keeper of Truth

One of the major roles of the church is to preserve the truth. "I am writing these things to you, hoping to come to you before long, but in case I am delayed, I write so that you may know how one ought to conduct himself in the household of God, which is the church of the living God, the pillar of support of the truth" (1 Tim. 3:14–15). The driving force behind the church is that it is the citadel of truth. That means that the church is to be known by the reliable, non-negotiating standard that operates dependent on the knowledge of God's Word.

The church is only to support those who are committed to the truth.

> If anyone comes to you and does not bring this teaching, do not receive him into your house, and do not give him a greeting; for the one who gives him a greeting participates in his evil deeds. (2 John 1:10–11)

Now let me compare that to 3 John 1:5–8:

> Beloved, you are acting faithfully in whatever you accomplish for the brethren, and especially when they are strangers, and they have testify to your love before the church. You will do well to send them on their way in a manner worthy of God. For they went out for the sake of the Name, accepting nothing from the Gentiles. Therefore we ought to support such men, so that we may be fellow workers with the truth.[1]

The second book of John talks about not receiving those into your homes who are not in line with the truth. The third book of John talks about receiving, supporting, housing, and encouraging those who are in line with the truth. He's saying in 2 John, give no audience to those who are not of the truth. It doesn't mean you can't talk to people who are confused about their faith. What he means is you cannot give an audience to people who are denying Christ. Regardless of the fact that they may have ten things that are true, if they are off about who Christ is, that is cataclysmic. That is nonnegotiable. The nonnegotiable is Jesus Christ. If you are confused about this issue or that issue, that is one thing. But the nonnegotiable is Christ. God would never negotiate that issue. That is the tests by which you measure whether you expose and get exposure to something.

On the other hand, he says in 3 John 1:7–8, "For they went out for the sake of the Name," (He calls Jesus, the Name), "accepting nothing from the Gentiles. Therefore we ought to support such men, so that we may be fellow workers with the truth." While you are not obligated to be involved with or to encourage those who bring untruth, you are expected to be vitally involved with those who carry the truth. But he now enters into the subject of the hospitality of the church that we are to be standing behind those men and women, those ministries that are carrying the truth.

He says you are to stand with them. You are to provide support for them. That you may be fellow workers with the truth. This concept of being a fellow worker, that's a powerful phrase. The idea is a joint participant. God has not called everyone to preach, but He has called every Christian to get behind the preached word. He's not called every Christian to be a missionary; but He has called every Christian to get behind legitimate missionaries.

> He who receives you receive me, and he who receives me receives him who sent me. He receives a prophet in the name of a prophet shall receive a prophet's reward, and he receives a righteous man in the name of a righteous man shall receive a righteous man's reward. And who ever in the name of a disciple gives to one of these little ones even a cup of cold water to drink; truly I say to you he shall not lose his reward.[2] (Matt. 10:40–42)

God just doesn't reward the preacher, the prophet, and the disciple. He rewards the one who becomes a fellow worker with the preacher, the prophet, and the disciple. The beautiful thing about it is even though you're not a preacher or a prophet, you can get their same reward because you stood with them in proclaiming the Name. Because you identify with them, supported them, enhance them, you made it possible for God's Word to go out. Their reward is shared with you. You are fellow workers.

I took a great deal of time talking about the truth because we share in what we support whether that is good or bad. Clearly, the context has to do with ministries that we support;

however, it also applies to what we support politically. For example, if I voted for a candidate that believed in the murder of babies in the womb, does God look the other way and say, "Well, that's politics and doesn't have anything to do with Me"? That is not the God of the Bible. You are delusional if you think that what you vote for (support in a candidate) is of no consequence to God. This book looks at multiple issues that God has spoken on. We are told that Jesus is truth, and God's Word is truth. There is a standard.

What I hear so often is, "Well, I know that the Bible says…but…" The problem with that statement is that it all depends on where you put your "but." Once you say that, the "but" negates the previous statements and what you are about to say has more authority than what the Bible has. The person is refusing to obey and apply the revealed Word of God. The bottom line is, what is your standard of truth? It is also not unusual that people do not apply the revealed Word of God. Let me illustrate with two stories from the Bible.

Chapter 13 of 1 Kings is about a young fireball prophet (preacher). The king was rebelling against God and the preacher said, "Thus says the Lord! Because you rebelled against Him, God is going to judge you." And he looked the king straight in the eye and said, "This is the truth." The Bible says he made the king so mad that the king reached out to grab the preacher and to take him into custody. But when he reached out his hand, his hand withered, and he drew back a nub. God judged the king for trying to punish the anointed one of God. The king realized his error and cried out to the preacher for mercy. The young preacher asked God to restore his hand, and God did restore his hand. The king, trying to show his gratitude to the young preacher, offered him a reward. The young preacher refused and told the king that God told him that he was to deliver the message, leave, and he was not to eat or drink anything until he arrived back home.

The Bible says in that town there was an older preacher. The old preacher had heard about what the young preacher had done. He was on fire for God, and he said, "Young preacher, you're going somewhere. Why don't you stay here with me and let me show you the ropes?" The young preacher said, "I can't do that. God told me to preach His word but not hang out in this neighborhood. God told me to leave here after I've done my business. I've got to go."

But then the old preacher said, "Young preacher, I was talking to God this morning, and God told me to tell you you're supposed to stay. Let's pick up the narrative in 1 Kings 13:18.

> He said to him, "I also am a prophet like you, and an angel spoke to me by the word of the LORD, saying, 'Bring him back with you to your house, that he may eat bread and drink water.'" *But* he lied to him.[19] So he went back with him, and ate bread in his house and drank water.

The young preacher thought about what the older preacher said God told him. So the young preacher changed his mind. Please stay with me. In order for the young preacher to go with the older preacher, he had to ignore God's revealed word. He apparently second-guessed God's revealed word, which was to go home and not to eat or drink anything at that place, fully knowing what God has said to him. He let an older preacher change his mind. So he stayed. But it was all based on a lie. Let's keep reading,

> Now it came about, as they were sitting down at the table, that the word of the LORD came to the prophet who had brought him back; and he cried to the man of God who came from Judah, saying, "Thus says the LORD, 'Because you have disobeyed the command of the LORD, and have not observed the commandment which the LORD your God commanded you, but have returned and eaten bread and drunk water in the place of which He said to you, "Eat no bread and drink no water"; your body shall not come to the grave of your fathers.'" It came about after he had eaten bread and after he had drunk, that he saddled the donkey for him, for the prophet whom he had brought back. Now when he had gone, a lion met him on the way and killed him, and his body was thrown on the road, with the donkey standing beside it; the lion also was standing beside the body.[3]

Please notice that God used the lying preacher again to pass judgment on the young preacher. That lets us know that

God can use a person, and then one minute later, they can be walking against God. But then, God can use them again, like He did with the old preacher. The point of the story is this: you better watch who you are listening to. Having a title in front of your name doesn't mean you should be listened to them. Just because you went to seminary doesn't mean you should be listening to them. You better watch who you are listening to. There's nothing wrong with listening to people; it's okay to listen to people as long as they are in line with the truth. It's okay to follow people. He says imitate those who are doing good and are in the truth. The young preacher allowed what someone said to negate God's revealed word. The danger of all of this is that because the young preacher refused to listen to God's revealed word, it cost him. And in this case, it cost him his life. Now I want to show you one from the New Testament that you are familiar with. It is found in Matthew's Gospel.

> Now when Jesus came into the district of Caesarea Philippi, He was asking His disciples, "Who do people say that the Son of Man is?" And they said, "Some *say* John the Baptist; and others, Elijah; but still others, Jeremiah, or one of the prophets." He said* to them, "But who do you say that I am?" Simon Peter answered, "You are the Christ, the Son of the living God." And Jesus said to him, "Blessed are you, Simon Barjona, because flesh and blood did not reveal *this* to you, but My Father who is in heaven.[4] (Matt. 16:13–17)

How do you think Peter was feeling after he heard Jesus tell him that his revelation was directly from God and not from man? He is probably feeling like he is all that, with a bag of chips and a cherry on top. After all, Jesus affirmed his confession and even said the church would be built upon that confession. Peter is probably a little cocky. Let's keep reading.

> "I also say to you that you are Peter, and upon this rock I will build My church; and the gates of Hades will not overpower it. "I will give you the keys of the kingdom of heaven; and whatever you bind on earth shall have been bound in heaven, and whatever you loose on earth shall have been loosed in heaven." Then He warned the disciples that they should tell no one that He was the Christ.[5]

Peter is still feeling pretty good about himself. Jesus is about to tell His disciples that He is going to Jerusalem to die, and then three days later, He will rise from the dead. Now watch what Peter does.

> From that time Jesus began to show His disciples that He must go to Jerusalem, and suffer many things from the elders and chief priests and scribes, and be killed, and be raised up on the third day. Peter took Him aside and began to rebuke Him, saying, "God forbid *it,* Lord! This shall never happen to You." But He turned and said to Peter, "Get behind Me, Satan! You are a

stumbling block to Me; for you are not setting your mind on God's interests, but man's."[6] (Matt. 16:21–23)

Look at the audacity of Peter. Verse 22 tells us that Peter pulled Jesus aside. Now keep in mind who Jesus is. Jesus is God in the flesh. Peter takes God aside and rebukes Him or chastises Him saying, "God forbid it, Lord!" Keep in mind that God had just revealed His word and will. His will from the foundation of the world was for Jesus to die for the sins of mankind and rise on the third day. Peter is chastising God and telling God that God (Jesus) does not know His own will.

Peter was feeling embolden because of his previous experience with Jesus telling him he was speaking for God. Yet five minutes later, Peter could not be further from the truth or the will of God. That is why we must pass our experiences through the grid of God's Word. Peter allowed his experience to ignore God's revealed word. God's Word has been revealed on all of the subjects listed in this book. Many Christians either ignore or they don't know what God has said on marriage, global warming, family values, the unborn, immigration, and so many other issues. Therefore, they don't see a connection to how they vote and what God will hold them accountable to when they stand before Him. I assure you, God is paying attention to what we support. He tells us that we will get their blessing or their curse when we support them.

Truth Is Knowable

Truth is knowable. We desperately, today, need to know what truth is. Author Alan Bloom said in *The Closing of the American Mind*, "It is now normative that any high school student or any college student will be taught in today's public education system with the thesis that truth is relative."[63] There is no fixed truth. It may be true to you, true yesterday, but it is not true today. Truth has become flexible, and there is no standard of truth. This has created a society that accepts no blame for anything. If you don't have truth, then you don't have to accept responsibility. A drunk driver that runs over someone, they say wait a minute, if they didn't put all that alcohol in the bottle, I wouldn't have gotten drunk. And I wouldn't have driven.

Everyone wants to blame somebody else. We have classrooms being run by students, because after all, it is not little Johnny's fault that he was raised without a father. And so we pass it on because there is no fixed standard of truth. Today we live in a world where there are no absolutes, and as a result of that, there is no God. In order to not have absolute, you have to get rid of God. Or you have to water Him down that he's not really God, He is just a religious concept because there is no truth. Where there is no truth there is no meaning, purpose, and you can't anchor anywhere because there is no final word.

A man takes out a gun, shoots his kids, and kills his wife, then shows his own meaninglessness by committing suicide. He's taking others with him. We live in a world today where we're all feeling the pain of no truth. Truth is no small issue. "You shall know the truth and the truth shall set you free" (John 8:32). He says there is such a thing as truth, and truth can be known.

What is the nature of truth? In John 18, Jesus is before Pilate to be judged. "I am not a Jew am I? Your own nation and its chief priest delivered you up to me, what have you done?" (Why are they so mad at you?) "Jesus answers, my kingdom is not of this world. If my kingdom where of this world, then my servants would be fighting, that I might not be delivered up to the Jews, but as it is, my kingdom is not of this realm. Therefore pilot said to Him, so you are a king?" (Pilate says to Jesus, "You really believe this, don't you?") "Jesus answered you say correctly that I am a king. For this I have been born, and for this I have come into the world." (The reason I came here is to be king. Now listen). "To bear witness to the truth. Everyone who is of the truth here's my voice."

What a statement. If you are of the truth, you listen to Me. Pilate said to him in verse 38, "What is truth?" You have got to be kidding. You mean to tell me you are here to represent the truth? What is truth? That's what we face today in college. Men don't know truth about manhood, women about womanhood, money, life, death, heaven and hell and God, or anything else. Nobody knows the truth, so to get around it and still sound sophisticated, they say, well, that's your opinion. We make truth relative and flexible so it doesn't offend anyone. When Paul preached, the results were either he started a revival or a riot.

So what do I mean when I used the word *truth*? I am telling it like it is. Truth means there is a body of information that corresponds with how things really are. We don't want our doctor writing prescriptions saying I think this is the right medicine. We don't want our pharmacists saying this looks like the color of the medication you wanted. We don't what our surgeons saying let's cut here and see what happens. You want somebody who knows what they are doing.

Prescribing your medicine, cutting you open, you want somebody who knows something about truth. Because you are assuming that truth is knowable that you can know how to do surgery or fill a prescription. But when it comes to God, it appears it is okay if nobody knows anything, or be flexible, or my opinion. So we're very inconsistent on truth. So what do we have, we have *agnostics*. Agnostics are those who say we cannot know truth. There are *rationalist* who say the only truth you can know is that which your brain can logically conceive. Rationalism is based on reason. We all know that doesn't work because we all have reasoned out things that we have made a mess of. Then you've got the idea that truth is really *subjective* and *personal*. You can't touch it, you can't grab it. This person says you can just feel truth. Then you have *positivism*, which says that the only thing that is true is that which the scientific method validates. Science has to be authenticated through hypothesis and data gathering.

Then you have *pragmatism*; it's true if it works. Then you have *realism*, which says there is a body of truth that is real, true, and you can know what truth is. There is an absolute standard of truth in the universe by which you can measure reality. Professors in every major secular university hold the position that truth is relative. One professor was going through all the various philosophical abstract information. He said we can conclude class, that there is no such thing as absolutes. Absolutes do not exist. A student's hand went up. "Teacher, I have a question. Are you sure there are no absolute?" "I am absolutely sure," responded the professor. To deny absolutes, you have to have an absolute because you have to say absolutes are impossible. So we cannot function without absolute.

Where do you find truth? How do I know who is telling the truth about the truth?

> Jesus spoke these things lifted up his eyes to heaven, he said Father, the hour comes, glorifying your Son, that the Son may glorify You; even as You gave Him authority over all flesh, that to all whom You have given Him He may give eternal life. This is eternal life, that they may know You. The only true God, and Jesus Christ whom You have sent.[7] (John 17:1–3)

So he says, "Father you sent Me, I'm over all mankind. My job is to deliver them to You. You are the only true God. How am I going to find out about Him?" John 17:17 says, "Sanctify them in the truth Your word is truth." There are three fundamental sources of truth. The first is nature. The Bible says the heavens and earth declare the glory of God. God is visible. Psalm 19:1–6 says even if you don't have the Bible you can see God. You can go anywhere in the world, and there will always be a consciousness of a supreme being even though they have never received a Bible.

God says He has written the Bible across the heavens. "The fool has said in his heart there is no God" (Ps. 14:1). In order to become an atheist, you've got to be a fool, which means you've been to college. "Always learning and never able to come to the knowledge of the truth" (2 Timothy 3:7). They may have many degrees, but they still don't have truth. The Bible says the fact that there is a God is obvious to all. You never find in the Bible God defending His own deity because a fool can see that God exists.

But then there's the Bible. That gives us another problem because a lot of people have their own holy books. Muslims have the Koran. Mormons have their own Bible. The Jehovah's Witnesses have their Bible. JT, you use the Bible, but other people use other books. How do you know that the Bible is the word of God?

Let's say that we don't know, for the sake of discussion, if the Bible is the right book or not. Let's just call it a history book. How do you know that George Washington lived? Do you know anybody that has seen George? No. We don't have videos of George. The only way you know George lived is that there is a record, a history book. But how do you know the record about George is a valid record? How do you know someone did not just make up the name George Washington and all the stories of his life? There's only one way you know: collaborating evidence. You don't have one book; you have other books and other people who saw George.

The more information you have, the more reliable the history book. The Bible is one book composed of sixty-six different books. The Bible was written over 1600 years by forty-plus authors. The Bible goes to great detail to let you know this is history. So we are not even talking about the supernatural. But let's just talk history. The reason why you have the Gospels is to let you know this is not just one person who saw Jesus. Matthew, Mark, Luke, and John all tell the same stories, and they talk about the same events.

God is letting you know this is history. Remember what John said in 1 John 1:1–5, "That which our eyes have seen, and our ears have heard, declare we onto you." John says we are personal eyewitnesses. You say wait a minute; what is your collaborating evidence? Do you remember having to read the classical Greek writers in college? Let me give you two classics. Nobody doubts that Homer wrote *The Iliad*.

The way we know he wrote the Iliad is because there are 643 copies. That lets us know he wrote the book. We say if there are 643 copies and his name is on it, he must be the author of the book.

We don't say I don't know whether Homer exists. Nobody doubts that Julius Caesar wrote *The Gallic Wars*. But we only have ten copies of that. But that's good enough if you have ten copies, Caesar must have written it. Guess how many copies of the New Testament we have—5,563. Everybody wants to doubt the Bible is real. They don't doubt regarding any other literature. Do you know why they want to doubt? Because the Bible says its author has to run your life. The reason why people don't want this book is because this book says that God Almighty is calling the shots. He is the creator, and people don't want that. Man would rather run his own life than to have somebody else tell him, "I am the truth, I am the way" (John 14:6), Jesus wants to run your life. It is the rebellion of man that will not take this book seriously.

Finally, the unique character in this history book is Jesus Christ. He skews the whole ball game. Muhammad said Jesus was a prophet. Muslims feel free to put Jesus and Muhammad beside each other. To the noncritical mind, they will look at that and say okay. No! Absolutely not, you can't do that. "Jesus said, 'Who do men say that I am?' 'Some say you are John the Baptist. Others say you are Elijah. Others say Jeremiah; others say you are one of the prophets'" (Matt. 16:13–20). They think you are a great guy, Jesus.

"But Jesus looked at them and said, 'Who do you say that I am?'" Most of us would hear he's a great prophet and would say yes. No! When you talk to a Muslim, they will say Jesus is a good prophet. If you ask them, "Can a good prophet lie?" They will say no. You can't be a good prophet and lie. Jesus said he is God. They will say, "Well, no, he is a good prophet." Well, if He says he's God and he's only a good prophet, then he lied. He can't be a good prophet. Which means Muhammad is wrong. But if he did not lie, and Jesus is who He said He is, Muhammad is still wrong because Jesus is not a good prophet—he is God. So Muhammad is wrong either way.

"And someone came to Him and said, 'Teacher, what good thing shall I do that I may obtain eternal life?'[17] And He said to him, 'Why are you asking Me about what is good? There is *only* One who is good'" (Matt. 19:16–17). Only God is good. Now who am I? Jesus says let's get this straight.

Micah 5:2 says Jesus will be born in Bethlehem. Micah 5:2 was written seven hundred years before Jesus was born. How did he know that unless the book is an accurate history book? And if it is an accurate history book with prophecy in the future, maybe it is a supernatural, very accurate history book. And if it is a supernatural, very accurate history book, then maybe its author is supernatural. And if it is a supernaturally, very accurate history book, whose author is supernatural, then it is the Word of God. Jesus said I am the way and the truth. He did not say I am a way, a truth. You have to read your articles when you read the Bible. Jesus says I am it, the alpha and omega (you run out of letters), beginning and the end, that's it. Christianity is not only supernatural, it is logical. It includes believing that the supernatural exist in order for the logic to work.

Finally, the benefit of truth. You say, "Okay, I believe there is a such thing as truth. So what?" "So Jesus was saying to those Jews who had believed Him, if you continue in My word, then you are truly disciples of Mine. And you will know the truth, and the truth will make you free" (John 8:31). Did you see that? He says truth can be known, not you shall guess the truth. As long as you're guessing, you will never be free. Not he shall think the truth. As long as you are thinking, you will never be free. Why are so many people in slavery today? They do not know the truth.

The Bible never lies. It never makes you feel good about the wrong in your life. It doesn't pat you on the back and say, "Well, everybody has problems." The Bible doesn't do that to you. It doesn't play psychological games that secular psychology plays with your mind. That's why the Bible can save you money. The Bible doesn't need two years of meetings to tell you the truth.

People hate you telling them you know truth. But if you know, then you know. He says that you might know the truth. Truth is knowable. College students don't let any professor tell you there are no absolutes because he's trying to override Jesus. Jesus says you can know the truth. You can know the truth about life, death, heaven, hell, sin, righteousness, marriage, family, money, and morality. And if you don't like it, it is still true. If you don't do it, it is still true. If you don't want it, it is still true. It is true because it is rooted in the true one, God. Truth has a foundation, and that foundation produces freedom. "You shall know the truth and the truth shall set you free."

There's all kinds of bondage in this world. There's human bondage that is slavery. You can have mental slavery. The reason why some of us are depressed is because we don't want to face the truth. So we want people to make us feel good about our confusion. So we will pay them $200 an hour to do it when the first step to overcoming your crisis is to deal with the truth. Truth is knowable.

But we cannot end without defining freedom. What is freedom? Freedom is not doing what you want to do. That is just an open door to a new kind of slavery. The drug addicts say "I want to be free to take drugs whenever I want" to take drugs. That's not freedom. Freedom is not doing what you want to do. Freedom is doing what you ought to do. If I am a fish in water, and I am tired of this water, what do I do? I've been in water for fifty-six years. I am sick of this water. I want to be free. I want to be free to go on dry land. I'm just tired of all this water. Let me go free. So I go down as deep as I can go, and I start wiggling my way to the top to shoot out of the water. I go up to the beach and looked up in heaven and say, "Free at last." Free at last, thank God Almighty I'm free at last.

Then it dawns on me, fool at last. Because I am not free if I am a fish and I get on dry land. Why? Because a fish was created to swim, and once I became something other than what I was created to be, I am no longer free. What am I now? I am dead. People want freedom to do whatever they want to do that is not freedom. That's why the Bible says don't do this, or only do this. God is trying to make you be free. But we say, "I want to be free." No, what you want is to be a slave of another kind.

Let's say I go to the piano because I want the freedom to play Bach, Mozart, and Beethoven. I walk up to the piano and say I'm free right now to put on a concert. The only way I am free to play Mozart, Beethoven, or Bach is that I've got to learn the rules. Without the rules, I'm not free to play the piece. Without God's rules, you are not free to live life as life was meant to be lived. You were created for God. And you can't play the piece called life unless you learn God's rules. God is right, and I am wrong every time, even when I don't like it, understand it, agree with it, or it seems illogical

Two farmers, Farmer Dale and Farmer Pete, would have a wager every year. One year they bet on a football game, or hockey game, or baseball game. This year they would bet on horses. So they each got their horse for the race. Farmer Dale always lost the bet to farmer Pete. Farmer Dale was determined that he was not going to lose this year. So Farmer Dale went out and hired a professional jockey to ride his horse to give him that winning edge.

The race began, and farmer Dale's horse took off like greased lightning. The professional jockey had him in line. Farmer Pete's horse was doing well despite the fact that he didn't know what Farmer Dale had done to him by getting a professional jockey. Farmer Dale's horse looked like he was going to take it hands down. The only problem was when they got into the stretch, the horses collided and fell down. So both horses and jockeys are lying on the ground. But the professional, having fallen before and knowing how to make adjustments, jumped up real quick, and he got on the horse and crossed the finish line.

Farmer Dale's jockey had crossed the finish line. Farmer Pete said, "Dale, you beat me this year." But then he looked over at Dale and he was upset. Dale was shaking his head, going crazy. Farmer Pete said, "What is wrong with you? I don't understand? Your man went over the finish line first. Why would you be upset?" Farmer Dale looked at him and said, "Because he got on the wrong horse."

People of God, watch what horse you are riding. Some people are riding "I'll wait until I become well-off then I will accept Jesus." You need to ride on King Jesus. If you ride on the wrong horse, you may get to the finish line thinking you made it over when you're on the wrong vehicle. Jesus Christ is the truth.

The following chapters deal with questions to ask any candidate about their belief system. The Bible speaks very clearly about what God says for us to do. When it comes to our political leaders, we are to follow the truth of God's Word in our selection process. That selection process gets cloudy when we, the body of Christ, do not know what God's Word says on abortion, same-sex marriage, global warming, excessive debt, parents being responsible for the raising of their children, and many other issues covered in this book.

The words of Ben Franklin, after the Revolutionary War was won, are appropriate to close this chapter:

> Have we now forgotten this powerful Friend? Or do we imagine we no longer need His assistance?… without His concurring aid, we shall succeed…no better than the builders of Babel; we shall be divided by our little, partial local interests; our projects will be confounded; and we ourselves shall become a reproach and a byword down to future ages.[8]

3

Christians Are to Vote on Economic Issues

Does the Candidate Know That God Expects You to Work and God Promotes Economic Self-Sufficiency through Work?

"For even when we were with you, we used to give you this order: if anyone is not willing to work, then he is not to eat, either" (2 Thess. 3:10). This passage is in the imperative mode. That means it is a command to work. In fact, Paul says if there is an able-bodied person and they decide not to work, Paul says to let them starve. It is not the church's responsibility to provide for someone who chooses to not work.

Follow this. A person comes to you and says, "I am hungry. I am not into working, but I am hungry, feed me." He may even use James 2:15–17: "If a brother or sister is without clothing and in need of daily food, and one of you says to them, 'Go in peace, be warmed and be filled,' and yet you do not give them what is necessary for *their* body, what use is that? Even so faith, if it has no works, is dead, *being* by itself." Or he might use

> Do not be surprised, brethren, if the world hates you. We know that we have passed out of death into life, because we love the brethren. He who does not love abides in death. Everyone who hates his brother is a murderer; and you know that no murderer has eternal life abiding in him. We know love by this, that He laid down His life for us; and we ought to lay down our lives for the brethren. But whoever has the world's goods, and sees his brother in need and closes his heart against him, how does the love of God abide in him? Little children, let us not love with word or with tongue, but in deed and truth.[1] (1 John 3:13–18)

They will say, "If you do not take care of me, I will starve." What does Paul say? "Then starve." You say that is hard. No, that is biblical because he is not talking about a person who cannot work. He is talking about a person who can work and should work but who will not work.

I have people come into my office all the time who try to make me feel guilty if I do not help them. They will say, "You are a pastor, you need to do this for me because the Bible says to help. You are supposed to be a Christian." So when I start asking them questions, they respond, "You don't need to know all that. Just do this for me." Yes, I do need to know all of that. You only told me one thing God said in His Word: help those who do not have. But that is not the only thing God said. God also says if they have the ability to work and they don't take advantage of that, don't help them. Let's deal with the entire Council of God and not just what we choose for our convenience.

God's Four Tiers of Responsibility

Paul uses a practical area here to talk about the issue of individual responsibility. The issue is not eating; it is symbolic of a larger issue. The issue is responsibility. Let me give you God's four tiers of responsibility. *Personal responsibility* is first. Do not go to anybody else to get them to do for you what you ought to do for yourself. You do not go to the government, you do not go to the church family, you do not go to your family; you go to yourself first. Personal responsibility is always first. That is reflected here. "If he will not work don't let him eat." Everything starts with personal responsibility. If you are unable to take care of yourself, then you go to the next tier.

Next is *family responsibility*. If there is a needy relative in your family who has a legitimate need, the family is supposed to take care of them. Do not bring it to the church at this time. Take it to your family first. "But if anyone does not provide for his own, and especially for those of his household, he has denied the faith and is worse than an unbeliever" (1 Tim. 5:8). Scripture says family responsibility is second. Scriptures teach that if you have the means, and your family member is doing all that they can to make ends meet, and they still are unable to make ends meet, you have a responsibility as a Christian to help them. Please note that the needy family member is doing all they can to make ends meet. If they are just trying to use you and are lazy, you have no obligation to help them. In fact, you will probably be interfering in the hand of God if you keep bailing them out.

Oftentimes there are chemical dependency issues or gambling issues that make it difficult to help the individual. One day I had a woman come in who asked us to pay her house note. As I began to inquire as to the circumstances leading up to her needs, it became obvious she was personally irresponsible. She was one of the few people who came to our church for needs that actually had more than $1,000 extra after paying all her bills. When I asked if she had a chemical dependency problem, she responded that she did not. I then asked her if there was a gambling problem (we had a casino about five miles away from our church). She told me, "Not anymore."

When I asked what she meant, she told me that last night was the last time that she was gambling and was not going to do it again. It turns out that she lost $1,100 last night at the casino and was not going to gamble anymore. She had all the money she needed to pay her bills, but she lost it all gambling the night before. Needless to say, we did not help her. If she is financially irresponsible, we are not obligated to assist someone.

Next is *church responsibility*. When you are doing all that you can as an individual, and when the family is doing all that they can and you are still unable to make ends meet, then the church comes along as God's extended family to assist. Chapter 5:4, 16 of 1 Timothy is the context of widows being placed on the list of assistance in the church. The Apostle Paul says, "But if any widow has children or grandchildren, they must first learn to practice piety in regards to their own family and to make some return to their parents; for this is acceptable in the sight of God…. If any woman who is a believer has dependent widows, she must assist them and the church must not be burdened, so that it may assist those who are widows indeed." If you cannot take care of yourself personally, and your family cannot help meet your needs, then the church is God's fallback position of assistance. In our founders days there was no such thing as government welfare. The church was the welfare system because they could hold people accountable.

After church responsibility comes the state or agencies. But the state is the last fallback position. That is the devastation of welfare. Welfare is telling people you don't have to be responsible, we will take care of you. Your family doesn't have to take care of you. In fact, if you bring a man in the house and do not marry him, we will still take care of you. This creates chaos, irresponsibility, and dependency. Today, we encourage people to be on unemployment for ninety-nine weeks, which creates an attitude of dependency. What I am about to say will be offensive; however, it is true. If you are an able-bodied person, capable of working, and you are on unemployment for ninety-nine weeks, then you are a thief. You are developing an attitude contrary to God's will for Christians.

You must realize that God takes work very seriously. Remember, before God gave Adam a wife and before the fall of mankind, God gave him two jobs. Yes, you heard me correctly—two jobs. "Then the LORD God took the man and put him into the Garden of Eden to cultivate it and keep it" (Gen. 2:15). Adam was to cultivate the earth and take care of the Garden of Eden. The second job was to name all the animals. "The man gave names to all the cattle, and to the birds of the sky, and to every beast of the field, but for Adam there was not found a helper suitable for him" (Gen. 2:20). After God gave Adam two jobs, then God gave Adam a wife.

> So the LORD God caused a deep sleep to fall upon the man, and he slept; then He took one of his ribs and closed up the flesh at that place. The LORD God fashioned into a woman the rib which He had taken from the man, and brought her to the man. The man said, "This is now bone of my bones, And flesh of my

flesh; She shall be called Woman, Because she was taken out of Man." For this reason a man shall leave his father and his mother, and be joined to his wife; and they shall become one flesh. And the man and his wife were both naked and were not ashamed.[2] (Gen. 2:21–25)

Ladies, here is a little side note: if the man you are seeing will not work, don't marry him. If you do, I can assure you that you will be in a miserable marriage and will regret that decision. God gave Adam a job, and he was happy to work. It was only after the fall of man that working became tedious because now there are weeds in the garden. The point of it is God has a chain of command, and you do not reverse the order. Most people reverse the order and go to the agencies or church first. When people come for assistance, they fill out our intake form, and it has all four of these categories on it. If in the interview I discover that they are not taking individual responsibility to meet their own needs, I don't help them. And not only that, I don't feel guilty about it. Remember, the standard is God's Word and not my emotional feelings.

Here is another thing to keep in mind. "For the poor will never cease *to be* in the land; therefore I command you, saying, 'You shall freely open your hand to your brother, to your needy and poor in your land'" (Deut. 15:11). This is what Jesus quoted in Mark 14:3–9:

While He was in Bethany at the home of Simon the leper, and reclining *at the table,* there came a woman with an alabaster vial of very costly perfume of pure nard; *and* she broke the vial and poured it over His head. But some were indignantly *remarking* to one another, "Why has this perfume been wasted? "For this perfume might have been sold for over three hundred denarii, and *the money* given to the poor." And they were scolding her. But Jesus said, "Let her alone; why do you bother her? She has done a good deed to Me. "For you always have the poor with you, and whenever you wish you can do good to them; but you do not always have Me. "She has done what she could; she has anointed My body beforehand for the burial. "Truly I say to you, wherever the gospel is preached in the whole world, what this woman has done will also be spoken of in memory of her."[3]

Jesus makes a point that the poor we will always have with us. The war on poverty will never end until Jesus establishes His millennium kingdom. We still have an obligation to assist when we can, but we must realize the poor we will always have with us.

In determining how we will help the poor, which Jesus encourages us to do, we cannot ignore Paul's command to the Thessalonians: "For even when we were with you, we used to give you this order: if anyone is not willing to work, then he is not to eat, either" (2 Thess. 3:10). If they are not willing to work, Paul says then they are not to eat. Again, we are not talking about someone who is unable to work; we are talking about someone who is not willing to work, and that is the difference.

God has three principles for handling money: give, save, and spend, in that order. Whenever you mix it up, you are out of God's will. You pay God, then you pay yourself, then you pay everybody else because we must learn responsibility. You never congratulate irresponsibility, you never support it, you never help it, you never encourage it, and you never pat it on the back. And most importantly, you do not let irresponsible people make you feel guilty for their irresponsibility.

You always promote responsibility, and you do not make others guilty to do for you what you can do for yourself. This is such a big issue because he says later in 2 Thessalonians 3:11, "For we hear that some among you are leading an undisciplined life, doing no work at all, but acting like busy bodies." If you do not occupy your time with the right things, you will occupy your time with the wrong things, being a busybody. A busybody minds everybody else's business but their own. They have too much time on their hands.

This must have been a big issue in the church. Paul says in verse 12, "Now such persons we command and exhort in the Lord Jesus Christ to work in quiet fashion and eat their own bread." In other words, leave my food alone. Believers were being misused in the name of the church. That was the problem. Paul has to command them to stand firm to force people to be responsible. Some of us, if we let them, our kids would live with us until they are fifty, having Mom still taking care of them. You have to do like the eagle does... kick them out of the nest. Let them stretch out their wings because it's time to fly!

Now Paul gets stronger. "But as for you, brethren, do not grow weary of doing good." What is the good he is talking about? He's talking about holding people responsible and standing firm. Look at what he says. "If anyone does not obey our instruction in this letter, take special note of that person [that means write his name down], and do not associate with him, so that he will be put to shame." I hear people say all the time you should not make people feel guilty. Why not? Guilt can be highly effective as a motivator. There is illegitimate guilt, and there is a legitimate guilty. Legitimate guilt is when a person does not take responsibility, and you make him feel guilty by saying we will have nothing to do with you anymore. Sometimes you have to do that with your own family members in order for them to become responsible.

You are saying to them, "Until you get your stuff together, we will not associate with you." That is very difficult, and that is why you have to stand firm because they will never learn as long as you keep giving in and bailing them out. They will never learn to be responsible. People ought to know that you are not going to associate with irresponsibility because God is creating a responsible church. God is calling on His people to be responsible. "Yet do not regard him as an enemy, but admonished him as a brother." He has not been kicked out of the church. He has not been viewed as a sinner. He is still a brother, but he needs a lesson. One of the ways that people get lessons is by disassociation or stepping away so they can hit bottom. He says there are some people in the Thessalonian church that you cannot associate with because their irresponsibility may rub off on you. Paul says to stand firm in the presence of God, and stand firm with the people of God. There are people to follow, and then there are people to avoid.

Will the candidate encourage the state to take the income of the earner and redistribute it to the nonearner? The Bible teaches we have different God-given abilities. The parable of the talents teaches us this principle. "For *it is* just like a man *about* to go on a journey, who called his own slaves and entrusted his possessions to them. To one he gave five talents, to another, two, and to another, one, each according to his own ability; and he went on his journey" (Matt. 25:14–15). Notice He gave them their talents based upon their abilities. It would have been foolish to give the last servant five talents because he would have wasted them. Will the candidate use the government to guarantee equality of opportunity for all and leave equality of result to individual drive, work ethic, abilities, and talent?

Does the Candidate Know
That the Bible Views the Family
as the Building Block for a Healthy Society?

It is not the government's responsibility to take care of your children. The family has always been at the core of every society; therefore, it is in the government's best interest to encourage, protect, and foster family integrity. In the creation of the United States of America, the family structure was different from that which was established in Europe. Alexis de Tocqueville, who traveled America to see what was created, did a comparison of the American family with that of European families. Here is how he described the differences:

> There is certainly no country in the world where the tie of marriage is more respected than in America, or where conjugal happiness is more highly or worthily appreciated. In Europe almost all of the disturbances of society arise from the irregularities of domestic life. To despise the natural bonds and legitimate pleasure of home is to contract a taste for excesses, a restlessness of heart, and fluctuating desires. Agitated by the tumultuous passions that frequently disturb his dwelling, the European is galled by the obedience which legislative powers of the state exact. But when the American retires from the turmoil of public life to the bosom of his family, he finds in it the image of order and of peace. There his pleasures are simple and

natural, his joys are innocent and calm; and as he finds that an orderly life is the surest path to happiness, he accustoms himself easily to moderate his opinions as well as his tastes. While the European endeavors to forget his domestic troubles by agitating society, the American derives from his own home the love of order which he afterwards carries with him into public affairs.[4]

According to de Tocqueville, when the society has no respect for the family, then the family deteriorates, then the society loses its moral compass. Our framers believed this wholeheartedly. They believed in the traditional roles of the family and its impact on how the society would function. They believed that both mother and father had equal responsibilities in raising children. John Locke's "Second Essay Concerning Civil Government" was written as the colonies were forming, and he speaks of parental authority in America contrast to Europe.

Seems so to place the power of parents over their children wholly in the father, as if the mother had no share in it; whereas if we consult reason or revelation, we shall find she has an equal title, which may give one reason to ask whether this might not be more properly called parental power? For whatever obligation Nature and the right of generation lays on children, it must certainly bind them equally to both the concurrent causes of it. And accordingly we see the positive law of God everywhere joins them together without distinction, when it commands the obedience of children: "Honor thy father and thy mother" (Exod. 20:12); "Whosoever curseth his father or his mother" (Lev. 20:9); "Ye shall fear every man his mother and his father" (Lev. 19:3); "Children obey your parents" (Eph. 6:1), etc., is the style of the Old and New Testament.[5]

The family provided solidarity in the home and stability in society. Locke believed that parental authority over children is a vital principle of natural law:

The power, then, that parents have over their children arises from that duty which is incumbent on them, to take care of their offspring during the imperfect state of childhood. To inform the mind, and govern the actions of their yet ignorant nonage, til reason shall take its place and ease them of that trouble, is what the children want, and the parents are bond to [provide.][6]

Locke felt that once the maturation process was complete, the child, now adult, would be capable of applying the revealed laws of God to his daily life. The children would have been raised to understand biblical principles and therefore function properly in society.

When he has acquired that state [of maturity], he is presumed to know how far that law is to be his guide, and how far he may make use of his freedom, and so come to have it; till then, somebody else must guide him, who is presumed to know how far the law allows a liberty. If such a state of reason, such an age of discretion made him free, the same shall make his son free too. Is a man under the law of England? What made him free of that law—that is, to have the liberty to dispose of his actions and possessions, according to his own will, within the permission of the law? A capacity of knowing that law, which is supposed, by the law, at the age of twenty-one, and in some cases sooner. If this made the father free, it shall make the son free too. Till then, we see the law allows the son to have no will, but he is to be guided by the will of his father or guardian, who is to understand for him… But after that [age of maturity is obtained] the father and son are equally free, as much as a tutor and pupil after nonage, equally subjects of the same law together, without any dominion left in the father over the life, liberty, or estate of his son.[7]

These principles are exactly what is taught in the Bible. The Apostle Paul goes into detail about marital and family relationships for a healthy home. Paul uses the word *submit*, which unfortunately has a bad connotation today. When Paul used the word *submit*, he had Jesus in mind. We must remember that Jesus submitted to the will of His Father when he came down to the earth. Look at the words of Paul from his letter to the Ephesians.

Wives, *be subject* to your own husbands, as to the Lord. For the husband is the head of the wife, as Christ also is the head of the church, He Himself *being* the Savior of the body. But as the church is subject to Christ, so also the wives *ought to be* to their husbands in everything. Husbands, love your wives, just as Christ also loved the church and gave Himself up for her, so that He might sanctify her, having cleansed her by the washing of water with the word, that He might present to Himself the church in all her glory, having no spot or wrinkle or any such thing; but that she would be holy and blameless. So husbands ought also to love their own wives as their own bodies. He who loves his own wife loves himself; for no one ever hated his own flesh, but nourishes and cherishes it, just as Christ also *does* the church, because we are members of His body. For this reason a man shall leave his father and mother and shall be joined to his wife, and the two shall become one flesh. This mystery is great; but I am speaking with reference to Christ and the church. Nevertheless, each individual among you also is to love his own wife even as himself, and the wife must *see to it* that she respects her husband. Children, obey your parents in the Lord, for this is right. Honor your father and mother (which is the first commandment with a promise), so that it may be well with you, and that you may live long on the earth. Fathers, do not provoke your children to anger, but bring them up in the discipline and instruction of the Lord.[8] (Eph. 5:22–6:4)

Since today's families are under stress, will the candidate increase this pressure through the added burden of taxation? Will he push excessive government regulation, which will spike consumer prices? Will he place employers under greater taxes and regulation leading to downsizing, layoffs, and the relocation of factories beyond America's borders? All of these increase financial stress upon the family unit.

Does the Candidate Know That the Bible Advocates Leaving One's Wealth to One's Descendants?

We must always remember that the government has no money but what they take from the people. The government's answer to their own financial irresponsibility is to come back to the taxpayers and take more of their hard-earned wealth. If one would look at all the taxes we pay throughout the year, it would boggle the mind. Uncle Sam does not trust us, that is why he takes federal withholdings before you see your check. If people would have to pay all their taxes on one day and not have it taken out of our checks or tacked on to our purchases, the government would see a whole lot less revenue.

When it comes to our children and our inheritances, the Bible speaks to these issues as well. Proverbs 13:22 reads, "A good man leaves an inheritance to his children's children, and the wealth of the sinner is stored up for the righteous." According to the proverb writer, a good man will leave an inheritance not only to his children but to his grandchildren as well. Our government has some of the most oppressive inheritance taxes that cripple families and, in some cases, causes them to have to sell or lose family farms and businesses. God expects us to leave an inheritance to our grandchildren and not to the government. It is our responsibility to provide for our families; however, the federal government makes it very difficult to accomplish that with despotic control of inheritance taxes.

The Apostle Paul lets us know that we are responsible for taking care of our family members. It is not the government's role to care for us or our family. Look what encouragement Paul provides the young preacher, Timothy, in his first Epistle. "But if anyone does not provide for his own, and especially for those of his household, he has denied the faith and is worse than an unbeliever" (1 Tim. 5:8). I want to know, will the candidate hinder generational wealth transfer with ridiculous inheritance taxes, which force the deceased's relatives to visit the undertaker and the IRS agent on the same day?

Does the Candidate Know That the Earth Experiencing the Cycle of Heating and Cooling and Global Warming Is a Hoax?

The world has been told that man is poisoning the atmosphere and is creating global warming. We are told that the scientist have a consensus agreement that global warming is real. We are told from the White House down that if you say that there is no global warming, there is something wrong with you, or you are a conspiracy lunatic. After a while, they no longer spoke of global warming, and now it is called climate change. Al Gore received a Nobel Peace Prize for his junk-science lie.

Global warming activist, John Cook, made a big media splash with the publication of a study by him and several coauthors claiming to prove that climate scientists overwhelmingly support the theory that human activity is warming the planet to dangerous levels. He claimed that 97 percent of scientists believe in global warming. It turns out that Cook cooked the books and made up the data. The media jumped on this as if it was the best thing since sliced bread. Even the White House announced the 97 percent support number for global warming.

> Out of the nearly 12,000 scientific papers Cook's team evaluated, only 65 endorsed Cook's alarmist position. That's less than one percent, not 97 percent.

Moreover, as we reported, the Cook study was flawed from the beginning, using selection parameters designed to weigh the outcome in favor of the alarmist position....In a May 22 (2013) follow-up article ("Climate *'Consensus' Con Game: Desperate Effort Before Release of UN Report*") The New American reported on additional problems with the Cook study and cited a large and growing list of eminent climate scientists—including Nobel Prize recipients and scientists who served on the UN's Intergovernmental Panel on Climate Change (IPCC)—who challenge the claim that there is any "scientific consensus" on climate change, or that "the science is settled" in favor of the Al Gore alarmist position....Now comes another devastating analysis of Cook's cooked data from a big name in the climate science community: Professor Richard S. J. Tol. Dr. Tol is a professor of the economics of climate change at the Vrije Universiteit in Amsterdam, Netherlands, and a professor of economics at the University of Sussex, England. He has also served on the UN's IPCC. Dr. Tol has statistically deconstructed the 97 percent consensus myth of Cook et al.[9]

Even Cook's e-mails revealed his scam ahead of time. He knew it was a scam before he even did the study. How do you know what the outcome will be before you do the study?

Populartechnology.net has posted e-mails from John Cook's Skeptical Science website concerning what Cook calls "The Consensus Project" or TCP. The e-mails, from early 2012, reveal the huge promotional campaign Cook was rolling out to publicize the consensus study—before he had even done the study. It is also evident from the e-mails that Cook knew he was cooking the data to reach a preconceived conclusion. In his "Introduction to TCP" e-mail of January 19, 2012, Cook explains to team members: It's essential that the public understands that there's a scientific consensus on AGW [anthropogenic (man-made) global warming]. So Jim Powell, Dana and I have been working on something over the last few months that we hope will have a game changing impact on the public perception of consensus. Basically, we hope to establish that not only is there a consensus, there is a strengthening consensus. Deniers like to portray the myth that the consensus is crumbling, that the tide is turning….Right from the get-go, it is apparent that Cook is planning to cook up a "game changing" study that will prove the "scientific consensus" he wants the public to accept. Typical of Cook and activists of his ilk is their use of "deniers" when referring to their opposition, an attempt to smear scientists who hold different opinions by equating them with Nazi holocaust deniers. It is hardly the mark of professional civility and collegiality one expects from true scientists.[10]

I want to use most of an article entitled "Global Warming Hoax: Leading Scientists Debunk Climate Alarmism." A group of sixteen world-renowned scientists decry the unscientific alarmism over global warming, citing numerous inconvenient facts that dispute global warming claims. They have a message for policy makers about global warming. It is a hoax. They put their names on the document.

> There is no compelling scientific argument for drastic action to "decarbonize" the world's economy. Even if one accepts the inflated climate forecasts of the IPCC, aggressive greenhouse-gas control policies are not justified economically….Every candidate should support rational measures to protect and improve our environment, but it makes no sense at all to back expensive programs that divert resources from real needs and are based on alarming but untenable claims of "incontrovertible" evidence.
>
> This statement follows up on the public resignation of Nobel Prize-winning physicist Ivar Giaever from the American Physical Society (APS) in which he states: I did not renew [my membership] because I cannot live with the [APS policy] statement: 'The evidence is incontrovertible: Global warming is occurring. If no mitigating actions are taken, significant disruptions in the Earth's physical and ecological systems, social systems, security and human health are likely to occur. We must reduce emissions of greenhouse gases beginning now.' In the APS it is

OK to discuss whether the mass of the proton changes over time and how a multi-universe behaves, but the evidence of global warming is incontrovertible?

The group of scientists note the following facts that refute climate alarmist claims:

1. The lack of global warming for well over 10 years now:

    This is known to the warming establishment, as one can see from the 2009 "Climategate" email of climate scientist Kevin Trenberth: "The fact is that we can't account for the lack of warming at the moment and it is a travesty that we can't." But the warming is only missing if one believes computer models where so-called feedbacks involving water vapor and clouds greatly amplify the small effect of CO_2.

    The lack of warming for more than a decade—indeed, the smaller-than-predicted warming over the 22 years since the U.N.'s Intergovernmental Panel on Climate Change (IPCC) began issuing projections—suggests that computer models have greatly exaggerated how much warming additional CO_2 can cause. Faced with this embarrassment, those promoting alarm have shifted their drumbeat from warming to weather extremes, to enable anything unusual that happens in our chaotic climate to be ascribed to CO_2.

2.   CO2 is not a pollutant:

   CO2 is a colorless and odorless gas, exhaled at high concentrations by each of us, and a key component of the biosphere's life cycle. Plants do so much better with more CO2 that greenhouse operators often increase the CO2 concentrations by factors of three or four to get better growth. This is no surprise since plants and animals evolved when CO2 concentrations were about 10 times larger than they are today. Better plant varieties, chemical fertilizers and agricultural management contributed to the great increase in agricultural yields of the past century, but part of the increase almost certainly came from additional CO2 in the atmosphere.

3.   The smear campaigns by the warming establishment are outrageous:

   Although the number of publicly dissenting scientists is growing, many young scientists furtively say that while they also have serious doubts about the global-warming message, they are afraid to speak up for fear of not being promoted—or worse. They have good reason to worry. In 2003, Dr. Chris de Freitas, the editor of the Journal Climate Research, dared to publish a peer-reviewed article with the politically incorrect (but factually correct) conclusion that the recent warming is not unusual in the context of climate changes over the past thousand years.

The international warming establishment quickly mounted a determined campaign to have Dr. de Freitas removed from his editorial job and fired from his university position. Fortunately, Dr. de Freitas was able to keep his university job.

4. Even if one accepts the inflated climate forecasts of the IPCC, aggressive greenhouse-gas control policies are not justified economically.

A recent study of a wide variety of policy options by Yale economist William Nordhaus showed that nearly the highest benefit-to-cost ratio is achieved for a policy that allows 50 more years of economic growth unimpeded by greenhouse gas controls. This would be especially beneficial to the less-developed parts of the world that would like to share some of the same advantages of material well-being, health and life expectancy that the fully developed parts of the world enjoy now. Many other policy responses would have a negative return on investment. And it is likely that more CO_2 and the modest warming that may come with it will be an overall benefit to the planet.

If elected officials feel compelled to "do something" about climate, we recommend supporting the excellent scientists who are increasing our understanding of climate with well-designed instruments on satellites, in the oceans and on land, and in the analysis of observational data. The better we understand climate, the better we can cope with its ever-changing nature, which has complicated human life throughout history. However, much of the huge private and government investment in climate is badly in need of critical review.

This is not the way science is supposed to work, but we have seen it before—for example, in the frightening period when Trofim Lysenko hijacked biology in the Soviet Union. Soviet biologists who revealed that they believed in genes, which Lysenko maintained were a bourgeois fiction, were fired from their jobs. Many were sent to the gulag and some were condemned to death.

The scientists then address the key issue of why there is so much intolerance and corruption among global-warming proponents, and the answer they give is sadly, "Follow the money."

Alarmism over climate is of great benefit to many, providing government funding for academic research and a reason for government bureaucracies to grow. Alarmism also offers an excuse for governments to raise taxes, taxpayer-funded subsidies for businesses that understand how to work the political system, and a lure for big donations to charitable foundations promising to save the planet. Lysenko and his team lived very well, and they fiercely defended their dogma and the privileges it brought them.

Signatories:

Claude Allegre, former Director, Institute for the Study of the Earth, University of Paris

J. Scott Armstrong, Co-Founder, Journal of Forecasting and International Journal of Forecasting

Jan Breslow, Head, Laboratory of Biochemical Genetics and Metabolism, Rockefeller University

Roger Cohen, Fellow, American Physical Society

Edward David, Member, National Academy of Engineering and National Academy of Sciences

William Happer, Professor of Physics, Princeton University

Michael Kelly, Professor of Technology, University of Cambridge

William Kininmonth, former Head of Climate Research, Australian Bureau of Meteorology

Richard Lindzen, Professor of Atmospheric Sciences, MIT

James McGrath, Professor of Chemistry, Virginia Technical University

Rodney Nichols, former President and CEO, New York Academy of Sciences

Burt Rutan, aerospace engineer, designer of Voyager and SpaceShipOne

Harrison H. Schmitt, Apollo 17 astronaut and former U.S. Senator

Nir Shaviv, Professor of Astrophysics, Hebrew University

Henk Tennekes, former Director, Royal Dutch Meteorological Service

Antonio Zichichi, President, World Federation of Scientists, Geneva.[11]

The science community is really echoing the words of the Bible. God is in control of heating and cooling of the earth. Genesis 8:22 reads, "While the earth remains, Seedtime and harvest, and cold and heat, and summer and winter, and day and night shall not cease." God says He is the one who placed heating and cooling cycles in the earth. We are told in Psalm 147:15–18 that God controls the weather. "He leads forth His command of the earth; His word runs very swiftly. He gives snow like wool; He scatters the frost like ashes. He casts forth His ice as fragments; Who can stand before His cold? He stands forth His word and melts them; He causes His wind to blow and waters to flow." It is God-ordained and not man-made. Global warming happened during the time of the Vikings, long before the SUVs and modern industry. Does the candidate attribute cycles of weather change exclusively to human activity? If he thinks it is man-made rather than God-ordained, he will likely favor increased government control and regulations over economic behavior, which can cripple an economy and have no impact upon global warming or cooling. Climate change is controlled by God and not by man.

Does the Candidate Know That the Bible Prohibits Stealing and Covetousness and Warns against Excessive Debt?

The Bible is not against debt, but excessive debt is a sin. The Bible gives warnings against stealing, and I maintain that what our government is doing is stealing from its citizens with excessive taxation. Our government is doing the same thing that Britain did to the American colonies before the Revolutionary War. "You shall not steal" (Exod. 20:15). "Render unto Caesar that which is Caesar's" (Matt. 22:21). The Bible says we are responsible and obligated to pay the legal designated taxes. Of course, government can steal by overtaxation. But it is immoral to overtax a population and use their hard-earned work and efforts to subsidize irresponsible government. An amazing amount of $240 billion a year is stolen by the American worker through the theft of time. You are committed to work eight hours, instead you only worked six even though you may be present for eight, and that becomes theft of time. When you steal time, you steal productivity; when you steal productivity, you still profit; and when you steal profits, then that is loss of revenue.

"The earth is the LORD's, and all it contains, the world, and those who dwell in it" (Ps. 24:1). God claims to be the only absolute owner. Everything else is management.

That is what we mean by stewardship. Stewardship is the protecting and the expanding of that which belongs to somebody else. Everyone is a steward. Now I know we use the word *ownership*—I own my house, own my car, etc.— and we understand what we mean. But from a theological perspective, you manage your car and your house; God has placed you in a managerial position over those things. You are not the ultimate owner because one day you will leave it, or it will leave you. Since God is the ultimate owner of the universe, then He gets to set the parameters by which the world is to operate. He says, "You shall not steal." He can say that because He owns it.

Stealing is a refusal to trust God to meet your needs. People steal because they do not trust God, because if you trusted God and knew who God was, you would not have to steal. "You shall not steal" was to force people to look to God to meet their needs. That means that in order for people to stop stealing, they must understand that God is their source for everything. For you to steal, that means you are your source because I am going to go get it, I am going to go take it, and I will make it mine. Once you claim to be your own source, then you are saying, "God, you are not my source." And then God will not be your source, and you will not get to experience the provisions of God.

One of the greatest things you can ever experience is seeing God supply when you cannot. Once you see that, you will never be the same because you know that you do not have to go out illegitimately to get something you want when you have God, who owns everything as your supplier. God is saying not to illegitimately seek to better your situation outside of God, because the moment you do, God will not be with you.

Habakkuk 2:6 says, "Woe to him who increases what is not his and makes himself [watch this], rich with loans." Buying things on credit that you cannot afford and you are unable to pay is a form of theft. Some of us need plastic surgery, cutting up the credit cards because we use them wrongly. There is nothing wrong with having them, but whenever we make ourselves sufficient by the use of borrowing for what you are unable to pay, we say, "I am trusting God that one day I am going to be able to pay my bills, so it is an act of faith to pull out the credit card at this time. That is what the Bible calls "tempting the Lord your God" (Matt. 4:7). The Bible specifically condemns that, and that is theft.

The answer to stealing is work. "He who steals must steal no longer"; stop stealing. Do not go to work tomorrow and steal anymore, including pens, paper, staplers, etc., "but rather," (instead of stealing), "he must labor, performing with his own hands what is good, so that he will have *something* to share with one who has need" (Eph. 4:28). The answer to theft is work; go out and get a job! That is what the Bible says. The question you are to ask if you need or want something is, How can I earn the resources to get it? God says you need to earn it. God says the answer to that is productivity, and that is why the Bible condemns laziness. Laziness is a person who does not want to earn it. He wants to take it because it is a lot easier to rob someone rather than to go to work because you can rob somebody in a couple of minutes.

> Here is what I have seen to be good and fitting: to eat, to drink and enjoy oneself in all one's labor in which he toils under the sun *during* the few years of his life which God has given him; for this is his reward. Furthermore, as for every man to whom God has given riches and wealth, He has also empowered him to eat from them and to receive his reward and rejoice in his labor; this is the gift of God.[12] (Eccles. 5:18–19)

This says God has given us work as a gift to be enjoyed. Now that enjoy part gets in the way because you say I am working, but I am working because I have to. That is because you have not connected work to your calling. If you disconnect work from your calling, then it becomes laborious. Let me tell you a little secret: it is better to make less doing something you are passionate about than to make more doing something you hate. The worst thing in the world I can ever conceive of is to spend every day hating to get up to go where you have to go to work. Paul's passion was preaching the gospel, but that could not fully support him, but he had a skill called tent making. So he would use his skill to fund his passion. So even if your job is not your passion, help it to fund your passion so that you are not living a passionless life.

"You shall not covet your neighbor's house; you shall not covet your neighbor's wife or his male servant or his female servant or his ox or his donkey or anything that belongs to your neighbor" (Exod. 20:17). At first glance, it sounds like the eighth commandment, "Thou shalt not steal." And while there is a correlation this commandment goes deeper, coveting refers to an illicit craving, leading to an illicit plotting to possess that which belongs legitimately to someone else, in this verse, your neighbor. It is a passionate longing to possess something that is not yours.

"You shall not steal" deals with the actual taking of it. "You shall not covet" deals with the passionate longing and pursuit of it, even if you never get it to own it. Please do not misunderstand this commandment. There is no condemnation in Exodus 20:17 for desiring to have your own. The condemnation is desiring to have that which is your neighbor. It is this uncontrolled lusting that can only be satisfied by either possessing it by theft or by plotting to possess it. The covetous person spends a great deal of time fantasizing, therefore, frustrated that the fantasy does not become a reality.

At the core of covetousness are both greed and materialism, greedy because it is not yours. When you say somebody is greedy, you are not only saying they want more of something, but they are saying I want what I do not have, and it becomes covetousness because what I want belongs to somebody else. Materialism is not that you have material goods or wealth. It does not refer to whether you have two cars or three cars, one house or five houses. There are many wealthy people in the Bible who God said He made them wealthy. So wealth in and of itself is not materialism.

Materialism is the foundation of covetousness. For the Christian, it is simply when the physical takes priority over the spiritual. It is when you define yourself by what you have. All of us know people who define themselves by what they have, and their significance is built into their stuff. The question we want to look at for the covetous person is often a materialistic person is this: If you lose your stuff, do you lose you? Not because things are unimportant, it is just things are never to be the most important. The covetous person who is also a materialistic person is regularly choosing gold over God.

They do not believe. "Then He said to them, 'Beware, and be on your guard against every form of greed; for not *even* when one has an abundance does his life consist of his possessions'" (Luke 12:15). He goes on to say what good is it to be rich in this life but not rich toward God. Materialism puts the physical before the spiritual. We think life would be so much better if I had more stuff. People can testify that more stuff does not solve your problems. Some of us today are making more money than we have ever made in our lives and are perhaps more miserable than we have ever been in our lives. We have more income, yet we are more in debt than we have ever been. That is because materialism born out of covetousness has only made our lives a mess: bill collectors, tranquilizers, and getting deeper in debt. This commandment was given to not destroy our lives.

The Apostle Paul gives us great insight into financial stability. Look at what he says to the young preacher, Timothy. "But godliness *actually* is a means of great gain when accompanied by contentment" (1 Tim. 6:6–10). Paul gives us the correct equation: Godliness plus contentment equals great gain. Many people have godliness, yet they are not content. There are many people who are content, but they are not godly. The proper equation is godliness plus contentment equals not just gain but great gain.

> For we have brought nothing into the world, so we cannot take anything out of it either. If we have food and covering, with these we shall be content. But those who want to get rich fall into temptation and a snare and many foolish and harmful desires which plunge men into ruin and destruction. For the love of money is a root of all sorts of evil, and some by longing for it have wandered away from the faith and pierced themselves with many griefs.[13]

He is not condemning having it, but he is condemning loving it. You say I do not love it, I just know I need to have it. Well, he gives us a test to determine if we love money:

do you have to compromise spiritually to get it, because if you do, then you love it.

This commandment was fundamentally given so that men would really see their sinfulness. The Apostle Paul says in Romans 7:7 I was good at keeping the commandment until I ran into the commandment you shall not covet. "What shall we say then? Is the Law sin? May it never be! On the contrary, I would not have come to know sin except through the Law; for I would not have known about coveting if the Law had not said, 'You shall not covet.'" He says once he ran into coveting, coveting jumped all over him. My sinfulness was revealed because I now wanted everything I could get my hands on. It revealed that I was not nearly as righteous as I thought I was because I was a covetous person. It revealed my spiritual problem is on the inside.

This commandment wants you to see that your relationships are more important than your stuff. Better is a smaller home with happiness than a bigger house with misery. But what we want is the bigger house despite the fact we're sleeping in separate rooms. All kinds of sins are wrapped up into this last commandment. Self-righteousness, self-pity, the covetous person feels sorry for themselves because they do not have it. They get jealous over the fact they don't have it, and they envy. Jealousy is, I am upset that you have it. Envy is, since I cannot have it, I want it. Envy says, I want to make you miserable too. This happens on the job; one person is jealous of another person, and so they gossip about their neighbor or put them down. That is jealousy that is turned into envy. That is why envy is often associated with strife—it leads to conflict.

At the core of this commandment is not to be covetous, it is really a positive thing and that is to trust God for what is mine. So I do not have to look for somebody else's. The covetous person concludes that God is holding out on me. If God was not holding out on me, then I would have that. So obviously God is not that concerned about me because they got a better house, a better car, and a better income. They have it, I do not. God, something is wrong with You. Covetousness says, God, you have made a mistake. The covetous person is never satisfied because they do not believe. "For the LORD God is a sun and shield; The LORD gives grace and glory; No good thing does He withhold from those who walk uprightly" (Ps. 84:11). Now let me tell you the disaster of covetousness. "Therefore consider the members of your earthly body as dead to immorality, impurity, passion, evil desire, and greed, which amounts to idolatry" (Col. 3:5). Coveting is idolatry. Do not miss that. Now go back to the first and second commandment, "You shall have no other gods before Me, you are not to make any graven images." We have come full circle; we are now back up to commandments no. 1 and no. 2. The principle is, if you have another god, then you cannot have the True Living God. And coveting is idolatry. Here is the point: the covetous person is actually blocking God from blessing him.

Many of us are standing in the way of our own blessings because we spent all of our time trying to get what belongs to somebody else. And since I am trying to get something that you were never meant to have, now God can't give you what He has for you because you have another god. Why? Because you are looking for things to provide for you what God wants to provide that will be your own. Now there is only one answer for this sin. It is a life-transforming answer, but it is a difficult answer.

We live in America, a place where you are free to dream. What makes America unique among the nations of the earth was its philosophy that men were created to be free. You can have life and liberty, and you can have the pursuit of happiness we give you the freedom to pursue your dreams. The problem with communism and socialism is the inability to pursue your dreams. Everything was government-mandated and controlled. In the Bible, government is supposed to be a small non-dictatorial supportive mechanism, not controlling. You are supposed to be free to pursue your life under God.

That is also our problem because freedom can be abused. When freedom is abused, people go after stuff for stuff's sake. We have got to be the only country in the world that has storage facilities that people rent to house things that your house cannot keep anymore. We pay rent to keep stuff.

Because we accumulate so much stuff, if you want to make some money and you have money to invest, build a storage facility because people accumulate stuff for stuff's sake. They accumulated stuff and pay rent to keep it.

God only has one answer for covetousness, and it is a life-transforming answer. If you get this answer, your life will never be the same. Many of the other problems in our lives are tied to our discontentment. Because we get discontent with life, it leads to all the other stresses in our lives. God's answer to coveting is simply contentment.

What is contentment? Does contentment mean I do not want to make any money, live in a larger house, drive a better car, buy a better suit, or move up the corporate ladder? Contentment is not a word that means stifle your dreams. I hope, as long as you have life and are in your right mind, you will never stop dreaming. Your life is to have purpose and a calling and reason. You are never to lose your dreams. Woe to the man or woman who has no dreams, because now all you are doing is existing, going from day to day and just repeating things.

Contentment does not mean that we can never talk about the goodness of God providing different things at different times in our lives. But what contentment does mean is inner satisfaction were I am until God blesses me with more. It means a sense of being satisfied. I am going to be at rest until the goodness of God gives me more.

> *Make sure that* your character is free from the love
> of money, being content with what you have; for He
> Himself has said, "I will never desert you, nor will
> I ever forsake you," so that we confidently say, "The
> Lord is my helper, I will not be afraid. What will man
> do to me?"[14] (Heb. 13:5–6)

He says, Let your character be free from loving money.
That means from having money have such a control over
you that the physical is more important than the spiritual.
He says the reason why you can be content with what you
have is because God says, I will never leave you nor forsake
you. To put it another way, God says, I have your back.

Yes, but, God, I am only in an apartment. God says, But
in that apartment I got your back. Yes, God, but I have an
old vehicle—but I got your back. Yes, God, but my money
is funny—but I have your income. God says, I have you.
Now if you do not believe that God has your back, you will
not be content; if you are not content, you will be covetous;
if you are covetous, you are an idolater. And God will not
have fellowship with other gods. So since God will not
fellowship with other gods, and covetous is another god,
you will not feel that God is with you. And you will not be
able confidently say he has got it. How do you know if you
are not content? Simple, you are not at rest where you are.

You always know a discontent person because they are
constantly complaining. Maybe you grew up in a home
where your mother cooked something that you did not like

that day. For me, that was liver. I think it should be a sin to make people eat liver. I have yet to find liver that the Lord has blessed. When liver was passed, I would say "no, thank you." At least I was polite. My dad would then take the liver, and he would cut a piece for me. And that was a mistake, because he always put more than I would have put on my plate. And then my dad would say, "And you better eat it all, and you better not complain." And then he would really mess with my head and become international, talking about somebody in India, China, or Africa who would love to have something on their plate to eat. I always wanted to say, "Well, box it up, and send it to them." But I didn't because I wanted to live to see twelve.

"Be anxious for nothing," (for how much? So anything that you are worrying about is illegitimate). "But in everything by prayer and supplication with thanksgiving," but God how could I be thankful for so little? How can I be thankful for not having enough? He is telling you not to be thankful for the negative situation. He is not saying be thankful your car is broken down or that the roof leaks. He is saying give thanks that you have a God that you can call upon in spite of the situation worrying you. "Let your requests be made known to God. And the peace of God, which surpasses all comprehension, will guard your hearts and your minds in Christ Jesus" (Philippians 4:6–7).

What do you give thanks for? Lord, I am stuck in this apartment, but I give you thanks because you know where my new house is located. I give you thanks that you are going to show me how to pay these bills. I give you thanks for what you are going to do. I thank you for who you are. In spite of where I am, I want to give thanks. I will thank you for hot dogs and bologna until you give me steak. I will praise you because I am not walking even if it is an old car. I will thank you that I have a job even though it is not the job that I desire. I will bless you because I have a God who is in control. In spite of your circumstances, be content. And the proof of your contentment is your thanksgiving, not in your complaining.

The national debt is stealing from our children and grandchildren. If you look at the National Debt Clock, you will see that we are above eighteen trillion dollars in debt, and that does not count the unfunded debt. We have created an atmosphere of envying what others have, which has led to coveting as a major sin in America. "The rich rules over the poor, And the borrower *becomes* the lender's slave" (Prov. 22:7). Unpaid debts is theft. "The wicked borrows and does not pay back, But the righteous is gracious and gives" (Ps. 37:21). Will the candidate continue to add to our runaway national debt? Increasing our national debt steals from future generations, but it also compromises America's economic well-being and national security.

The Founding Fathers saw debt as the evil for what it is. Ben Franklin once said, "Think what you do when you run in debt; you give to another power over your liberty." When we borrow, we are pledging against the future. We are looking at the immediate advantage, only to be indebted in the future with obligations not only for what was borrowed but with considerable interest. The bottom line is, debt robs you of your freedom and makes you a slave to the lender. Thomas Jefferson wrote:

> The maximum of buying nothing without the money in our pockets to pay for it would make our country one of the happiest on earth. Experience during the war proved this; and I think every man will remember that, under all the privations it obliged him to submit to during that period, he slept sounder and awoke happier than he can do now.[15]

The founders believed that debt should be hated like the plague. They believed that the debt of those in office should be paid for before they left office. Unfortunately, in American history, there has only been one president who left office without debt, and that was Andrew Jackson. Thomas Jefferson felt inherited debt was immoral:

> That we are bound to defray [the war's] expenses within our own time, and unauthorized to burden posterity with them, I supposed to have been proved in my former letter....We shall all consider ourselves morally bound to pay them ourselves; and consequently within the life [expectancy] of the majority....We must raise, then, ourselves the money for the war, either by taxes within the year or by loans; and if by loans, we must

repay them ourselves, proscribing forever the English
practice of perpetual funding.[16]

We are the first generation that is actually squandering
the next generation's inheritance. Our excessive debt is a
crime. We will never be able to pay off our debt, and it is
growing in leaps and bounds. May God have mercy on our
souls. Our spending is like a junkie looking for his or her
next fix. Our only hope is to go through withdrawals, just
like a junkie, to clean ourselves of our spending addiction.
We must stop the wasted spinning, and we must cut to ever
have a chance of being debt-free.

Does the Candidate Know
That the Bible Teaches
That the Alien Immigrant
Must Obey the Law of the Land?

Many people are surprised to discover that the Bible
speaks about aliens in the land. It is important for us to
understand what an alien is according to the Scriptures.
This section on alien immigration comes from the book
The Immigration Crisis: Immigrants, Aliens, and the Bible by
James K. Hoffmeier. Most of this section is his words. I
highly recommend you read his book. The Hebrew word,
usually translated "stranger," "alien," or "sojourner," comes
from the verb *ger*, which occurs eighty-one times in the Old
Testament. It means "to sojourn" or "to dwell as a stranger,

become a refugee." This same word, *ger,* is used as a noun eighty-two times in the Old Testament. With more than 160 references to the term *alien* lets us know how prevalent this word is in ancient Israel.

It is very difficult to get a handle on this word because it is translated in different ways in different passages. Yet the same word is used. The Hebrews had a completely different word for the word *foreigner*: *nekhar*. Many times this particular word has been interchanged with the word for *alien*, and that is unfortunate. The two words cannot be confused. The word *ger* and *nekhar* refer to two different categories of people. That is why it is critical to understand the biblical definition of an alien and how one attain that status is very important, because advocates of illegal immigration are using passages from the Old Testament to support their position as if the English word *alien* and the Hebrew word *ger* have the exact same meeting.

Christians for Comprehensive Immigration Reform (CCIR), on the sojourner's Web site, quotes Leviticus 19:33–34, which states, "When a stranger [*ger*] resides with you in your land, you shall not do him wrong. The stranger who resides with you shall be to you as the native among you," and based on this scripture declare, "We are working together to revise comprehensive immigration reform as soon as possible, because we should share a set of common moral and theological principles that compel us to love and care for the stranger among us."[1] CCIR has a compassionate concern for aliens, but does the word *ger* (ie, aliens, sojourner, and stranger) apply to immigrants regardless of their legal standing?

When Abraham approached the residents of Hebron to purchase a burial plot for his wife, Sarah, who had just died, he identified himself as "an alien and a stranger" (Gen. 23:4), or "an alien and a settler." The word *alien* (*ger*) is sometimes combined with the term *resident* (*toshav*, literally "one who resides"); this is the word Abraham used. The two terms together literally means "resident alien." This means they have essentially taken up permanent residency in a foreign land, as Abraham and his family had done in Hebron, with the permission of their host. In fact, the people of Hebron acknowledged Abraham's status as being one who is "among us" (Gen. 23:6), rather than viewing him as a foreigner (*nekhar*). This indicates not only that the aliens (*gerim*) have resided with the host nation for a period of time, but that they have abandoned their homeland for political or economic reasons and sought refuge in another community. In other words, the *ger* regards the land of his sojourning as the new home for a lengthy time period while the foreigner does not.

In biblical days, the foreigner is one who travels to a country or is there for business purposes. One of the reasons why the aliens required a host or patron was because they would not be a part of any kinship group and thus would lack protection. That is why the meaning "protected citizen" can also be applied to the word *ger*. The alien is a guest of sorts, and as such, the alien was not entitled to offer hospitality to others. That would be like me inviting someone into my home, and it is not appropriate for that visitor to invite other people to come into my home. The alien had to get permission from the host country to bring others into their home.

The alien was a permanent resident. The foreigner, on the other hand, was not. For the most part in Israel, foreigners were those who were passing through the land with no intentions of taking residents, or perhaps they would be temporarily seasonally employed. In the Bible, the foreigners and the alien were not the same, and they should not be confused. They actually had different standings in the community. In the Hebrew Bible, the alien was people who entered Israel and followed legal procedures to obtain recognized standing as a resident alien.

When you think of the story of Joseph, you see some principles about aliens that come to the forefront. Joseph was sold into slavery by his jealous brothers and he was a foreigner in the land of Egypt. But Joseph attained to a very high position based upon his competency, and the fact that God's hand and anointing was upon him. Joseph was able to assimilate culturally and with the language without forgetting his mother tongue. He took an Egyptian name, and he married an Egyptian woman (Gen. 41:45). Joseph had become so Egyptionized that when his father, Jacob, died in Egypt, Joseph ordered him to be mummified; that was an Egyptian practice. When Joseph died, he was mummified, and his remains were placed in a coffin (Gen. 50:26), again another distinctive Egyptian custom and not used by the Israelites after they settled in the Promised Land.

As you know the story of Joseph and the children of Israel migrating to Egypt (Gen. 46–47), from their statements, we can learn about aliens. Joseph lived in Egypt and was a high-ranking official in the court of Pharaoh. You will recall that when his brothers came for grain, Joseph had so acclimated himself and assimilated himself into the Egyptian culture that his brothers did not recognize him. This happened twice in the Genesis narrative. He dressed the part, his language was Egyptian, his behavior was Egyptian. Joseph had become Egyptian. He had to receive permission to bring his father, Jacob, to Egypt, along with the rest of his extended family. In fact, Pharaoh offer them the land of Goshen in the northeastern delta as a place to graze their flocks and herds.

> Now when the news was heard in Pharaoh's house that Joseph's brothers had come, it pleased Pharaoh and his servants. Then Pharaoh said to Joseph, "Say to your brothers, 'Do this: load your beasts and go to the land of Canaan, and take your father and your households and come to me, and I will give you the best of the land of Egypt and you will eat the fat of the land.'"[17] (Gen. 45:16–18)

When his family arrived in Egypt, Joseph presented them to Pharaoh. "Then Joseph went in and told Pharaoh, and said, 'My father and my brothers and their flocks and their herds and all that they have, have come out of the land of Canaan; and behold, they are in the land of Goshen.'² He took five men from among his brothers and presented them to Pharaoh" (Gen. 47:1–2). Five of Joseph's brothers make a request to Pharaoh in Genesis 47:4: "They said to Pharaoh, 'We have come to sojourn in the land, for there is no pasture for your servants' flocks, for the famine is severe in the land of Canaan. Now, therefore, please let your servants live in the land of Goshen.'" The phrase "sojourn in the land" is the verb *ger* that is followed by the words "live in the land," which is the word for *resident* (*yashav*). What they are asking is if they can be a resident alien in the land of Egypt. This is the same request that Abraham made in Hebron in Genesis 23. The brothers were invited to live in Egypt by Pharaoh himself, but the brothers felt compelled to ask formally for permission to settle as resident aliens with their families. Genesis 47:5–6 lets us know that Pharaoh granted the request. "Then Pharaoh said to Joseph, 'Your father and your brothers have come to you. The land of Egypt is at your disposal; settle your father and your brothers in the best of the land, let them live in the land of Goshen; and if you know any capable men among them, then put them in charge of my livestock.'"

Please notice that the Hebrew immigrant asked to receive permission to enter a foreign land and, in this case, from the great king himself. Please notice also that in Genesis 47:3, "Then Pharaoh said to his brothers, 'What is your occupation?' So they said to Pharaoh, 'Your servants are shepherds, both we and our fathers,'" Pharaoh is asking about their occupation. It is interesting that in Genesis 47:1–6, there are four references to flocks and herds of the family. Apparently the king did not want a group of people to enter Egypt to become financially and economically dependent upon the governmental resources. The mere fact that they make reference to the livestock shows that they did not intend to be a burden on the state.

> The same law shall apply to the native as to the stranger who sojourns among you. (Exod. 12:49)
>
> There shall be one standard for you; it shall be for the stranger as well as the native, for I am the LORD your God. (Lev. 24:22)
>
> *As for* the assembly, there shall be one statute for you and for the alien who sojourns *with you,* a perpetual statute throughout your generations; as you are, so shall the alien be before the LORD. There is to be one law and one ordinance for you and for the alien who sojourns with you.[18] (Num. 15:15–16)

Please note that the law for the alien and the law for the citizen are to be the same. We start with obeying the law.

If someone is here illegally, they have already disobeyed the law. God expects those who reside in a country to obey the laws of that country. Will the candidate vote for laws that the citizens are to follow and then vote for exemptions for himself and his staff (ie, The Affordable Health Care Act known as ObamaCare)?

The reason why this is important is because in ancient days, there was no equal justice under the law. For example, people were classified as priests, citizens, lower-class groups, and slaves. Penalties for the very same crime differ depending upon what social class you were in. And in many cultures, the alien was not even mentioned as a legally protected group or individual in the laws. This was evident in the Code of Hammurabi and other Mesopotamian legal documents.

God did something very radical in the Bible because the biblical laws for legal aliens were for them to have legal protection, just the same as a native-born Israeli. On the other hand, the aliens were subject to the same regulations, and if they were guilty of an offense, the same justice was doled out against them. That is what is meant by the same law applies to the native-born and the alien in Exodus 12:49. While the alien was to be treated in an equal manner legally, the expectation was for foreign residents to adhere to all the rules and regulations of Israelite law. Simply put, they were to receive equal protection under the law, but they were also equally responsible to respect and uphold the laws in its totality. Aliens could not ignore certain social laws because they differed from those of their native culture, or because they disagreed with an aspect of Israelite law. They could not pick and choose the laws that they would obey and yet remain in good standing with the Hebrew people.

King Hezekiah included the aliens in one of his crowning achievements when they celebrated Passover as a national event in Jerusalem. The story is written in the book of Chronicles.

> Then the whole assembly decided to celebrate *the feast* another seven days, so they celebrated the seven days with joy. For Hezekiah king of Judah had contributed to the assembly 1,000 bulls and 7,000 sheep, and the princes had contributed to the assembly 1,000 bulls and 10,000 sheep; and a large number of priests consecrated themselves. All the assembly of Judah rejoiced, with the priests and the Levites and all the assembly that came from Israel, both the sojourners who came from the land of Israel and those living in Judah. So there was great joy in Jerusalem, because there was nothing like this in Jerusalem since the days of Solomon the son of David, king of Israel. Then the Levitical priests arose and blessed the people; and their voice was heard and their prayer came to His holy dwelling place, to heaven.[19] (2 Chron. 30:23–27)

Aliens were included in this special celebration. What is significant about this is that this is five hundred years after the Exodus, and it shows that the religious inclusion intended for the alien was being taken seriously. The inclusion of the alien in the Passover illustrates God wanted aliens to be residents of His salvation, provided they follow the provisions laid out in the law for their incorporation into the community of Israel.

The kings of Israel were to base their kingship on the legal materials in the law of the Torah. In fact, Deuteronomy demands that the king have his own copy of the law and read it!

> Now it shall come about when he sits on the throne of his kingdom, he shall write for himself a copy of this law on a scroll in the presence of the Levitical priests. It shall be with him and he shall read it all the days of his life, that he may learn to fear the LORD his God, by carefully observing all the words of this law and these statutes, that his heart may not be lifted up above his countrymen and that he may not turn aside from the commandment, to the right or the left, so that he and his sons may continue long in his kingdom in the midst of Israel.[20] (Deut. 17:18–20)

Not only was the king to have a copy of the law, he was to live by the laws himself and not consider himself above the law. Again we see that the law applies to all. Congress has no right to make laws for those of us in the land and then exempt themselves from the very laws or the mandate that we follow. It is an abomination in the eyes of God.

When the kings failed to promote justice, Jeremiah actually went to the palace to confront the king and his officials and the people.

> Thus says the LORD, "Go down to the house of the king of Judah, and there speak this word and say, 'Hear the word of the LORD, O king of Judah, who sits on David's throne, you and your servants and your people who enter these gates. Thus says the LORD, "Do justice and righteousness, and deliver the one who has been robbed from the power of *his* oppressor. Also do not mistreat *or* do violence to the stranger, the orphan, or the widow; and do not shed innocent blood in this place. 4"For if you men will indeed perform this thing, then kings will enter the gates of this house, sitting in David's place on his throne, riding in chariots and on horses, *even the king* himself and his servants and his people. 5"But if you will not obey these words, I swear by Myself," declares the LORD, "that this house will become a desolation."21 (Jer. 22:1–5)

Please note that the Prophet said: doing wrong and violence against the alien is one of the things that caused the Babylonian captivity. Obedience to God's commandments was a condition of remaining in the Promised Land. The threat of the destruction of the land and exile hung over Israel's head. The kings were to uphold the law and see that justice was done. When the king of the nation deviated, the prophets swung into action. The prophets of today are the preachers in America. Where are the preachers calling the nation to repentance?

An interesting note is that while the children of Israel were in Babylonian captivity, the Jews were never called aliens. Instead, they were called exiles, and they certainly were exiled to Babylon. You might naturally wonder why they were labeled exiles and not aliens. Certainly they were residing in a foreign land, but they had been taken to Mesopotamia by force; thus they were prisoners of war. Remember, an alien in ancient Israel was one who resided in a foreign land, by choice, with the permission of the host nation.

From this information, we can learn some significant information about aliens in the Scriptures. First, aliens had to get permission from the host country in order to be admitted. That means, from the very beginning, they were being obedient to the laws of the land. That is a significant statement; because what is going on with our border today is a crime. It appears that there is no rule of law to be followed. Next, as we learned from Joseph, he assimilated into the culture. That means he learned the language, he dressed appropriately for that culture, and he even adopted an Egyptian name. Joseph truly became Egyptian, yet he was able to continue to maintain his own Hebrew identity. You recall when his brothers came to visit to get grain he understood them, but they did not understand him.

I believe that citizens and aliens and foreigners should be subject to the nation's laws, and this applies to immigration laws and how we enter a country and become a legal resident or citizen. Every country in the world has laws like this, and the reason is to promote an orderly society. Why is it that we think that American laws should be set aside, but we do not feel the same thing about other nations laws? In December 2013, I was in the country of Israel. As a visitor, I was required to obtain an entry visa in order to get into the country. Typically, a country will limit how long a visitor can stay in their country. I obeyed the laws of the land while I was visiting the beautiful country of Israel. Just because I was a Christian did not excuse me from their laws. I am obligated to submit to the laws even if I do not like them or think that they are unfair or inconvenient.

Some people say that we should have an open border because we are all made in the image of God. Well, just because people are made in the image of God, a government official or authority should not look the other way when a crime is committed. There is no basis in Scripture for such a stance. The mere fact that we are made in the image of God shows that God has expectations of humans. That is why people who believe in the Bible as a source of authority should be held to a higher standard. Governments are ordained by God, and laws and ordinances made by humans, unless they clearly violate God's principles or teaching, should be followed.

Equal justice under the law applies to the alien and citizens alike in Israel. The laws of the Bible were to be equally applied to citizens and aliens. Cities who offer sanctuary for illegal aliens do so without the support of biblical law. Biblical sanctuary was only intended to allow the innocent party to get a fair hearing in trial and not for the purpose of sheltering lawbreakers from the authorities and agents of the state. Cities that provide a safe haven for illegal immigrants, while intended to be a gesture of justice, are, in fact, violating federal law and are misappropriating biblical law.

The law was specific that the aliens who were living with you must be treated as one of your native-born (Lev. 19:34) and therefore was eligible for social benefits (Lev. 19:9–10; Deut. 26:12–13). As in biblical law, the legal alien should receive the same social benefits as a citizen. However, as the law of the gleaning lets us know, the poor and the aliens actually have to go out and work in the fields to get grain and fruit (Lev. 19:9–10, 23:22; Deut. 24:19–21). Even the Bible expected people who were receiving assistance to do something to meet their own needs. They had to go work the field.

There were also consequences for disobeying the laws of the land. In fact, when Abraham lied to the Egyptian authorities about his marital status and in the identity of Sarah, his wife, he was expelled from Egypt. Again, this goes back to the very simple principle of obeying the law. One thing to keep in mind as you study this issue of immigration is that nowhere in the Old Testament is there any sense that a nation had to accept immigrants, nor was being received as an alien a right. That just simply did not exist in the Scripture. Permission was required for a foreigner to reside in another land as we saw with Jacob's family and Joseph. The alien in the Bible was a legal alien that had rights within the Israeli society that were denied to the foreigner. In the Bible, it is legally and morally acceptable for a government to deal with those in the country illegally according to the nation's legal laws.

How is it that in my great state of Oklahoma, that my nephew from Texas (an American citizen) would have to pay more to attend one of our institutions of higher education than someone who is here illegally? Illegal aliens pay less in tuition than legal citizens from other states. Again, we must obey the laws of the land. When I am in a foreign country, I must obey their laws or suffer the consequences.

Let me give you some statistics about illegal immigration that will help put this issue in perspective:

- $11 Billion to $22 billion is spent on welfare to illegal aliens each year by state governments.[22]

- $22 Billion dollars a year is spent on food assistance programs such as food stamps, WIC, and free school lunches for illegal aliens.[23]

- $2.5 Billion dollars a year is spent on Medicaid for illegal aliens.[24]

- $12 Billion dollars a year is spent on primary and secondary school education for children here illegally, and they cannot speak a word of English![25]

- $17 Billion dollars a year is spent for education for the American-born children of illegal aliens, known as anchor babies.[26]

- $3 Million Dollars a DAY is spent to incarcerate illegal aliens.[27]

- 30 percent of all federal prison inmates are illegal aliens.[28]

- $90 Billion Dollars a year is spent on illegal aliens for welfare and social services by the American taxpayers.[29]

- $200 Billion dollars a year in suppressed American wages are caused by the illegal aliens.[30] The argument is that the illegal aliens are doing jobs that Americans won't do. I have a friend with a masonry business that pays his workers a fair wage. He is often under bided by those who pay their workers under the table. They are not doing jobs Americans won't do.

- The Dark Side of Illegal Immigration: Nearly One million sex crimes are committed by Illegal Immigrants in the United States.[31]

The total cost is a whopping $338.3 billion dollars a year. That is enough that could have easily set up a medical account for the forty million Americans without insurance to have been given a one-million-dollar account and still have money left over to stimulate the economy. That would have been a much better alternative than the Affordable Health Care Act (a.k.a. ObamaCare). So…what can we learn? Aliens should assimilate into the culture of America, learn the language, and be productive citizens who obey all off the laws, just like a citizen of the country. If they want to become a citizen, they should go through the proper legal channels, and if not, they should be deported.

Alien immigration could have been placed in all three categories of economic issues, social issues, and foreign affairs issues. I placed it in economic issues because it has, in my opinion, the greatest impact on the economy, which impacts social issues as well as foreign affairs.

4

Christians Are to Vote
on Social Issues

Does the Candidate Know
That the Bible Makes No Distinction
between the Born and the Unborn?

"For You formed my inward parts; You wove me in my mother's womb" (Ps. 139:13). "Before I formed you in the womb I knew you, And before you were born I consecrated you; I have appointed you a prophet to the nations" (Jeremiah 1:5). Pro-lifers believe that life begins at conception. However, if you look at the words that God said of Jeremiah, God views life beginning before conception. Does the candidate favor legal protection for the unborn, or will he continue the slaughter of the unborn?

"You shall not murder" (Exod. 20:13). This commandment concerns the sanctity of human life. Life has value. It assumes the uniqueness of human life as in our constitution the wish for life, liberty, and the pursuit of happiness. Our Founding Fathers understood that you could not pursue happiness unless you were free to do so and had life. So if you kill life, then you kill liberty, and you kill the pursuit of a meaningful existence. So at the foundation, everything you want to do is an assumption that you are alive to do it. "You shall not murder." That means that there can be no unauthorized executions of another individual. It is not your decision to make.

The word *murder* meant some sort of homicide. God did authorize certain taking of life in the Bible. The Bible allows for self-defense, the Bible allows for the government to enact capital punishment. "You shall not murder" means there can be no unauthorized life-taking unapproved by God.

The implication of life removes all "cides." That means there cannot be any suicides, the taking of your own life. Every suicide recorded in the Bible, the person was out of the will of God when they took their lives. Not only is suicide a problem but patricide, the killing of father; matricide, the killing of a mother; fratricide, the killing of a brother; sororicide, the killing of a sister; infanticide, the killing of a baby; genocide, the killing of a race; or feticide, the killing of a fetus. All cides are in violation of this commandment (you shall not murder) because that is unauthorized by God. The reason why the sixth commandment exists is because you are uniquely created in the image of God. The worst thing about evolution, other than the fact that it will make a monkey out of you, is that you lose your dignity. All you are is just part of progressive order, and you are not distinct, and you are not unique. You are just evolving. But God's Word would differ from that assessment. Man was unlike anything that God made because it is the only thing that God made that He did so in His own image.

You have the stamp of God on you. You are not just another part of the animal kingdom. Therefore, murder in any form unauthorized by God is to attack God. You have to understand, to attack any individual in the image of God and murder on any level is to attack God because the individual bears the image of God. Genesis 9:6 puts it like this: "Whoever sheds man's blood, by man his blood shall be shed, For in the image of God He made man." That is, you have been given something that animals and plants do not have, and that is the spiritual nature of God residing in you. We have souls, spirit, and immaterial nature all men are created with it and are unique. We are different.

Human life was set apart in creation by a divine pattern in God's image because we were given a purpose, and that is dominion. It is an awesome thing. God says, I am going to give you the stewardship to run this planet, I want you to rule it on my behalf, and I am going to give you the right of dominion. If you do not think that is who you are, you will not act like that. The reason why a lot of people act like animals is because they think like animals. Their dignity has been ripped from them, and they do not understand. So they lose their conscience and ability to make correct decisions because they don't know who they really are.

There is no place where this has been more violated than in the area of the unborn. Abortion is not the killing of a fetus but the killing of an unborn child. You must understand abortion is murder, the illegitimate taking of a life, which is why in order to legitimize it, they have to say it is not a life, because if you kill it, then that is murder. So if it is not a life, then you did not really murder because it was just tissue. When Elizabeth was six months pregnant with John the Baptist, Mary, her cousin, had just conceived Jesus by the Holy Spirit and visited her.

> Now at this time Mary arose and went in a hurry to the hill country, to a city of Judah, and entered the house of Zacharias and greeted Elizabeth. When Elizabeth heard Mary's greeting, the baby leaped in her womb; and Elizabeth was filled with the Holy Spirit. And she cried out with a loud voice and said, "Blessed *are* you among women, and blessed *is* the fruit of your womb! "And how has it *happened* to me, that the mother of my Lord would come to me? "For behold, when the sound of your greeting reached my ears, the baby leaped in my womb for joy.[1] (Luke 1:39–44)

The Bible says when Mary was pregnant with child, not with tissue, so God views the unborn fetus as a life, as a baby, not as something that is disposable.

> If men struggle with each other and strike a woman with child so that she has a miscarriage, yet there is no *further* injury, he shall surely be fined as the woman's husband may demand of him, and he shall pay as the judges *decide.* But if there is *any further* injury, then you shall appoint *as a penalty* life for life, eye for eye, tooth for tooth, hand for hand, foot for foot.[2] (Exod. 21:22–24)

You are to receive equal recompense for their lives because God views them as life. Let us get this straight; the reason why the unborn baby is a life is because the unborn baby possesses the image of God. Once the conception has occurred, the image of God enters the process. And once the image of God enters the process, an attack on the fertilized egg is an attack on God.

What happens when people murder any of the "cides?" God has established a guideline. He says if you murder, you shall have your life taken from you. That is called capital punishment. The Bible says capital punishment is biblical. Not kind of biblical, it is very biblical. But the punishment cannot be an act of an individual; it is only acted upon by the court. The government can do it, individuals cannot. It has to be the government or the courts.

At this point, I hear many of you yawning, and you are saying this is boring because I am not murdering anybody, and I am not thinking about murdering anybody. All of us have committed murder. Matthew 5 lets us make this more relevant. "You have heard that the ancients were told, 'You shall not commit murder,'" (Jesus is saying. You heard what the Old Testament said. You shall not commit murder). "And 'Whoever commits murder shall be liable to the court.'" This is where the courts come in because the court has to respond as a legalized agent. The Old Testament gives the minimal standard of divine expectation. So if you never stabbed or shot anybody, you have met the minimum responsibility. Jesus now takes us deeper. "But I say to you That everyone who is angry with his brother shall be guilty before the court; [wait a minute; you are going to take me to court because I am mad? The answer is yes.] And whoever says to his brother, 'You good-for-nothing,' shall be guilty before [watch this] the supreme court"; (we have gone from the local courts now; we are at the Supreme Court), "and whoever says, 'You fool,' shall be guilty *enough to go* into the fiery hell" (Matthew 5:21–22). Oh no, he didn't go there.

Jesus said the fact that you have not shed any physical blood, you have met the minimum standard, but I say unto you, the definition of murder goes deeper than that. Jesus says, "My definition of murder goes deeper than just the physical." It is when you use your mouth to bring destruction to another person because you are angry; you have committed spiritual murder. What you are doing is murdering their character and their opportunity. So you are not necessarily shedding blood, but you are destroying. So my question to you is, are there any murderers reading this book?

All too often we just mention abortion, and we never talk about what it is. This section will be a little bit graphic. One of the ways that an abortion is done is by sticking a knife inside the womb and cutting off the head, the arms, the legs, and cutting the torso in half. After that, a vacuum cleaner is inserted to suck out all the pieces; after that, they take inventory to make sure that the mother does not get an infection from any pieces that were left behind. A second way abortions are done is by injecting a saline solution into the womb. As the baby ingests the solution, it begins to burn the inside of the child and simultaneously burns the outside of the child's skin. In about forty-eight to seventy-two hours, the child is born dead, usually. A third way is a partial birth abortion in which, as the child is being born, the doctor snips the spinal cord while the child is still in the womb with his head outside of the womb so that the baby cannot survive.

One of the main arguments that women use to defend abortions is to say, "You cannot tell me what to do with my body." One of the problems with that statement is, "Honey, it was not your head that they cut off! It is that of an innocent child." My question has always been, how is it that a Christian can support abortion? Does a Christian think that when they stand before God that God is going to pat them on the back and say, "Well done, good and faithful servant. Enter into your rest." Do they think that God is going to be pleased with how they had mutilated human life? Do they think that they are going to get a pass because it is just tissue and not a human being as we are being told? Some men consider life beginning at conception, but God considers life beginning before conception, as with Jeremiah 1:5.

We abort children because they are an inconvenience in our lives. Perhaps we do not have time for them. We need to adopt the mindset of God. The Scriptures make it clear that children are a blessing from the Lord. They are not an inconvenience, they are not a burden, they are not a tax deduction; they are a blessing from the Lord. Psalm 127:4–5 reads, "Like arrows in the hand of a warrior, So are the children of one's youth. How blessed is the man whose quiver is full of them."

Since *Roe v. Wade*, we have killed over fifty-eight million babies in the United States of America in the name of freedom of choice for mother. Do you really believe it is a woman's choice to chop off the head of her baby? As I said, I know this is graphic for the most part, but people do not even talk about what abortion is. One day, as I was sharing about the way abortions are performed, I had a middle-aged woman say to me that she did not like what I was saying because she did not actually know what abortions were. That is the reason why we need to talk about abortion. Proverbs 6:17 tells us seven things that the Lord hates, and one of them is "And hands that shed innocent blood." We have shed the blood of the innocent, and it is displeasing to God.

In the black community, the statistics are heartbreaking. America only contains 12 percent black population.[3] At the same time, 40 percent of all abortions are performed on blacks in America. In New York City, there was a billboard that was forced to be taken down because it was reported to have been racist. The poster showed a young black girl, and the caption read, "The most dangerous place for an African-American is in the womb." The reason for that is that in New York City, today, 59.8 percent of all black babies are aborted.[4] That is 60 percent of the black population; that is genocide. The great tragedy is black people are voluntarily taking our children to be slaughtered.

How is it that the church is sitting on the sidelines and saying nothing about this? This is a horrendous crime here in America. There are thirty-six million blacks in America, yet today we have killed more than sixteen million black babies.[5] That is 44 percent of the population! Forty-four percent of the black population in America! More American black babies have been killed by abortion since 1973 than the total number of Americans black deaths from AIDS, violent crimes, accidents, cancer, and heart disease combined.[6] Does your heart break as mine does? Do you think that God's heart is breaking? Are we not as Christians supposed to be allowing the things that break God's heart to break our hearts? Are we not to allow the things that cause God's heart to rejoice for our hearts to rejoice? Again, I asked the question, how can a Christian support this? How does a person who claims to know and serve God think this is okay?

Years ago, a dear friend told me of a dream she had. She said she dreamed she saw a vision of God sitting on His throne and seated at His right hand was Jesus Christ. When she panned the audience, there were millions upon millions of babies who were interceding for their parents who aborted them, the doctors who performed the abortions, the judges who made the laws, the politicians who created the legislation, and the governors who signed the laws. They were asking God to be merciful and forgive them. She was deeply moved when Jesus left His Father's side and joined the children on His knees interceding and pleading their case.

One of our political parties makes abortion one of the planks of their platform. That means this is what they stand on. So what is it that they are standing on? They are standing on the bodies of dead babies (they are standing on severed heads and limbs and think it is okay) in the name of political expediency so they can get votes. There is nothing easy about this subject. It is a vile, evil black eye on America that should cause us all to be ashamed of ourselves.

Does the Candidate Know That God Has Established Heterosexual Monogamy as the Pattern for Marriage?

God defined marriage long before there was a United States of America. Government did not establish marriage, therefore it cannot define or redefine it.

> Then the LORD God said, "It is not good for the man to be alone; I will make him a helper suitable for him." Out of the ground the LORD God formed every beast of the field and every bird of the sky, and brought them to the man to see what he would call them; and whatever the man called a living creature, that was its name. The man gave names to all the cattle, and to the birds of the sky, and to every beast of the field, but for Adam there was not found a helper suitable for him. So the LORD God caused a deep sleep to fall upon the man, and he slept; then He took one of his ribs and closed up the flesh at that place. The LORD God fashioned into a woman the rib which He had taken from the man, and brought her to the man. The man said, "This is now bone of my bones, And flesh of my flesh; She shall be called Woman, Because she was taken out of Man." For this reason a man shall leave his father and his mother, and be joined to his wife; and they shall become one flesh. And the man and his wife were both naked and were not ashamed.[7] (Gen. 2:18–25)

God is the one who said that it was not good for man to be alone. So when he created a helper for man, He created a woman and not another man. God established monogamy as the pattern for marriage in the book of Genesis. So the question is, will the candidate promote this divine standard as the societal norm, or will he view it as one among many lifestyle alternatives?

History started in Genesis 1:1. "In the beginning God…" This tells us that the universe is not a chance happening. We are not all evolving from some sort of slime or one-celled ameba or a big bang theory. Evolution is nothing more than man's way of trying to figuring out his environment so he doesn't have to deal with God.

God wanting to put His stamp on creation in a unique way creates man, the crown jewel of His creation.

> Then God said, let Us make man in Our image, according to Our likeness; and let them rule over the fish of the sea and over the birds of the sky and over the cattle and over all the earth, and over every creeping thing that creeps on the earth. And God created man in His own image, in the image of God He created him; male and female He created them. And God blessed them, and God said to them, "Be fruitful and multiply, and fill the earth, and subdue it; and rule over the fish of the sea and over the birds of the sky and over every living thing that moves on the earth.[8] (Gen. 1:26–28)

Man is created to have dominion over the earth. You must understand that before family, comes purpose. The purpose was that mankind would have dominion. When you get to family and marriage, that just makes possible a process to achieve a command to have dominion: manage God's creation. Stewardship is the management of God's creation. The idea is for man to rule under God.

Remember, the fall of man has not occurred…yet. Man is still in a perfect environment. "And God saw all that He had made, and behold, it was very good. And there was evening and there was morning, the sixth day" (Gen. 1:31). So when God created mankind, He created the capstone of His creation, whose job it is to run His creation. God not only creates man, He gives him managerial responsibility. Chapter 1 says man was made in God's image. Chapter 2 explains the process. Why? Because the coming to be of man was different than the coming to be of animals. Don't let a scientist lie to you and tell you that you are just another form of an animal. That's the ultimate insult because animals are not made in the image of God—we are.

In Genesis 2:18, the woman comes on to the scene, and she will also be made part of this period of probation. "Then the Lord God said, it is not good for man to be alone, I will make him a helper suitable for him." Woman is conceived in the mind of God, not Adam. Adam wasn't out girl-watching. Please note that this is different than the creation of male and female animals. Male and female animals were all created at the same time. Male and female human beings were created at different times. The reason why this happened is because male and female human beings were given the responsibility of dominion, animals were not. And whenever you have dominion, you have to have hierarchy. You have to have a way to get it from one group to another.

So God doesn't tell Eve what God told Adam. God tells Adam and tells Adam to tell Eve because Eve is Adam's responsibility. Adam is God's responsibility. So if Adam doesn't listen to God, Eve doesn't know what is happening. And if Eve doesn't listen to Adam, then there is a breakdown in the family structure. So that you will find out that Cain and Abel doesn't listen to Eve, and it flows down and led to disastrous results.

God said I am going to make Adam a helper. All right, ladies, once you are married, your priorities change. There is no sin in the world at this time. So whatever God is saying about women, it is as perfect as the environment in which God is saying it. And He says, "I am going to create Eve for one specific purpose: to assist Adam." The way she was going to assist him was coming alongside of him and working with him.

Men, it is important that you understand that Adam knew his calling. He knew that a confused man makes a confused family. I don't know how many ladies have told me, "I don't know where he wants to go. He doesn't have any direction." Men, your directionlessness keeps her off balance. So women will create their own direction if you don't. Just a side note, single ladies, any man whose direction you can't follow, you should not marry him because you are going to be very frustrated, and you will not fuse into his calling.

"Adam gave names to all the animals…but for Adam there was not found a helper suitable for him" (Genesis 2:20). Adam knows now, after naming all the animals, that something is missing. He sees that for every Mr. Bear, there is a Mrs. Bear. For every Mr. Crocodile, there is a Mrs. Crocodile. But there is no Mrs. Adam. And none of those creatures that he had named would work. Something was missing.

Now what this says, men, is that it is not wrong to need a woman. There is no sin in the world, and this man needs a woman. The more mature you get, the more you see that you can't do it alone. And that is why you need a helpmate. A man is a fool who does not use the expertise of his wife to help him accomplish God's calling on his life. God is not asking women to give up their knowledge, intellect, abilities, and skills. He is not asking them to become dumb now that they are married. But He is asking them to use their skills to merge into one calling. She is not to use her skills for her own individualistic calling anymore. She has got to merge those skills and abilities that God has given her on her family. That's the difference. You don't give up the skills, but you do merge them. You are willing to place it under a new hierarchy system.

"So the LORD God caused a deep sleep to fall upon the man, and he slept; then He took one of his ribs and closed up the flesh at that place" (Gen. 2:21). Eve is created out of Adam. So Adam is only half the man he used to be because he loses one side. In order for him to become a whole man, he has to get his rib back. But his rib is now located in somebody else. He can't take the rib out of somebody else and put it back. So in order to get his rib back, he has to take hold of somebody else's life and make this somebody part of his life to get the rib back that he lost. But getting his rib back means he gets another half he didn't count on. Because he not only gets his rib, he gets her rib too.

So what marriage does is bring back what you lost with a bonus. That is why she is different from you. That means, ladies, if you are going to understand your rib, you have got to understand Adam because half of your ribs belong to him. So in order for you to understand who you are in the marriage relationship, you need to understand who he is, because half of what makes you *you* is part of what makes him *him*. So in order for both of you to become all that both of you were meant to be, both of you have to merge into each other. Both of you must use your ribs and each other's ribs to form the original rib that got lost in the first place.

If you don't take from your mate their strengths, you do not become all you were created to be. God performs the marriage ceremony, and Adam says, "This is now [he doesn't say she is now. He says, "This is now," meaning this new relationship, he is talking about marriage] bone of my bone, flesh of my flesh, she shall be called woman because she was taken from man" (Gen. 2:23). Adam names her. He names her after himself. His name in Hebrew is *Eish*. The Hebrew word for *woman* is *Eisha*. In the first marriage, she takes his name. All Eve knows when she is created is that she is there. She doesn't know who she fully is until she receives his name. That is why in marriage, there is a transfer of names from the woman's last name to the man's last name, because she is now merged into another purpose.

Ladies, before she was married, she wasn't upset and frustrated. She didn't open up her eyes and say, "God, where is my man?" When she was created, all she knew was where God was. So if you have to wait for a man, you got to know where God is. Because if you don't know where your man is and you don't know where God is, you don't know where you are. God has created every woman to be with some male, either a man or God until a man. God has never asked a woman to be without a male supervisor that is directly God, or God's vice president, man. Until God transfers you to a man, God wants you transferred to Him. That is why the Bible says in 1 Timothy 5:3–16, if you have a widow in the church, she has to do one of two things: she has to seek marriage or commit herself to God for the rest of her life. She must be under some male pattern authority in order for her to achieve all of God's purposes for her life.

"For this cause a man shall leave his father and mother" (Gen. 2:24). It is not a woman leaves her father and mother. Why, because a woman transfers security. When you hand over your daughter to be married, you are transferring security. Therefore, you must transfer her to someone who will at least give her as much security as you will. She doesn't have to leave her father and mother until there is someone who is as secure as her father and mother. "Man leaves his father and mother [to become the new block of security], cleave unto his wife [making a new base for security and then harmony], and they shall become one flesh."

"And the man and his wife were both naked and they were not ashamed" (Gen. 2:25). They were not naked because they were not sinless. They were naked because they were children; they were brand new on the scene. The Bible does not relate lack of clothes to sin. The Bible says God has a robe. But He is perfect. So sin and clothes do not necessarily go together. They were simply naked because as far as creation was concerned, they were children.

The man and woman have gotten married, but a decision has not been made about the two trees: the tree of life and the tree of the knowledge of good and evil. It goes back to the commandment. Eat of every tree. Don't eat of this tree. And God says I will wait until you decide. There is great danger in delaying obedience because when God says do something and you don't do it, it is going to get harder to do it. And what you do is what the New Testament calls, "Creating an opportunity for the devil" (Eph. 4:27).

When children don't obey their parents immediately, they set themselves down a road where disobedience becomes easier until it is time to pay the price tag, which could be catastrophic. Because there is a promise that goes with obedience to parents, or lack of obedience to parents, that can determine the rest of your life. Parents, there is a promise that goes with obedience to God. What Adam should have done the day he got married, he should have said, "We are going to have our honeymoon dinner. You come with me, honey, and let's mosey on over to the tree of life, bite this pear, or apple, and seal this baby for the rest of our lives." Is that what he did? No!

Let me tell you what he did. He let the woman run the home. Listen to me, men. Men say, "I got to go to work, you run the home. The OKC Thunder are playing, you run the home. The Sooners are playing, you run the home. Whatever you say is fine with me." That is all the devil needed. The devil (in Genesis 3:1) walks up to the woman and says, "I'd like to talk to you. Do you know anything about horticulture? I want to talk to you about what God told you about trees." Satan never mentions the tree of life. All he wanted to talk was about how stingy God was on the tree of good and evil. The worse part is that Adam was listening to the conversation.

Most people think that Adam was off somewhere tending the garden. Adam wasn't off anywhere, because when you get to Genesis 3:6, it says, "And the woman ate and gave." There is a flow from her to him. There is not a time flow, only a movement flow. The man sat there and let the devil talk to his wife. He let the devil tell her how to run his family. That is always the issue in the family: will the devil run it, or will God run it? One of the great tragedies that we are facing today is role reversal where the woman is running the family, taking the lead. The woman is setting the pace. And all Dad can say is, "Ask your mother."

They never got around to the tree of life, and you know what that meant? Once they ate of the tree of the knowledge of good and evil, probation was over. Test failed. No biting the tree of life. They were out because Adam refused to run things like God wanted them ran. God comes walking and says, "Adam, where are you?" He should have come looking for Eve and said, "Eve, you should not have been talking to that devil."

No, no, no. When the family breaks down, the issue is always Adam. God says, "Adam, I made you and told you, you are in charge. The buck stops with you! She may have been wrong, but I am looking for Adam. Doesn't mean Eve was right. But, Adam, you are supposed to be controlling your family."

Just like Eve shouldn't follow Adam if he is leading her wrong, Adam shouldn't follow Eve if she is doing the same thing. Adam should have said, "Eve, you don't talk to another man about my family. I don't recall when we had devotions last night, me inviting the snake to get into the discussion of my business. This is my family." In fact, what he should have said is, "Excuse me, serpent, but I didn't invite you to my dinner table. I don't need no other brother talking to my wife. Get up out of my house." That is what he should have said. But he had become sissified or feminized. What he wanted to do was sit back and watch his wife be happy. He wasn't a leader.

Why did God create marriage and family? There are six purposes. The first reason is *procreation*: having babies. The Bible makes grand statements about having babies. The more the merrier. Why the big deal? Remember God told Adam and Eve to be fruitful and multiply so that you will have dominion over the earth. The reason was not just to have people that looked like them, it had to do with the theology of dominion. Dominion meant to reproduce yourself and spread out all over the earth so that all over this planet, there would be somebody ruling under God's authority. Babies are a way to make sure that the name of God gets perpetuated throughout the entire earth. Most of us have babies to carry our name. God says to have babies to carry His name everywhere.

Secondly is *self-realization*. "Adam, I will make a helpmate for you." That is another way of saying, "Boy, you need help. You are incomplete." As long as you are single,

God is your completeness. When it is time to marry, God is in the process of bringing someone along to fix up the rest of us to make us complete. The reason Adam was given a wife was to complete him. God doesn't give you somebody just like you. For if both of you are the same, then one of you would be unnecessary. He gives someone who is different from you so that you can make up the difference, so that you can fulfill the complete purpose of God that He has ordained.

Third is *divine illustration*. You are a type of Christ in the church. The Bible says that you are the bride, and Christ is the bridegroom. You are to illustrate a greater reality of God to His people. So a bad marriage means a bad illustration. So when you get divorced, you are saying something bad about God. Ephesians 5:32 tells us that this is an illustration of the relationship of Christ.

Fourth is *companionship*. God created marriage for companionship. "Then the Lord God said, 'It is not good for the man to be alone'" (Gen. 2:18). There is a great blessing in sharing life with the one you love—your companion. God created Adam and Eve and not Adam and Steve when He declared that it was not good for man to be alone.

Fifth is *enjoyment*. God created sex for enjoyment, in the context of marriage. "Stop depriving one another, except by agreement for a time, so that you may devote yourselves to prayer, and come together again so that Satan will not tempt you because of your lack of self-control" (1 Cor. 7:5).

Outside of the context of heterosexual marriage, there might be "pleasure for a season," but there can be no true, lasting enjoyment.

Sixth is *protection*. God desires a godly seed. "But not one has done *so* who has a remnant of the Spirit. And what did *that* one *do* while he was seeking a godly offspring? Take heed then to your spirit, and let no one deal treacherously against the wife of your youth" (Mal. 2:15). God knows that marriage provides protection for the family.

The book of Romans gives us a description of the end-times society when Jesus will return, and God will pour out His wrath upon that society. That society is the breakdown of the family. Let us take a peek at that society. "For the wrath of God is revealed from heaven against all ungodliness and unrighteousness of men, who suppress the truth in unrighteousness." (Now here is what the wrath of God is poured out upon.) "Because that which is known about God is evident within them; for God made it evident to them. For since the creation of the world His invisible attributes, His eternal power and divine nature, have been clearly seen, being understood by what has been made, so that they are without excuse." What is that saying? That says that there is no excuse for anyone to not know that God exists. They can conceive the creation of God in its beauty, in its orderliness, and in its systematic nature.

"For even though they knew God, they did not honor Him as God, or give thanks; but they became futile in their speculations and their foolish hearts were darkened. Professing to be wise they became fools." I have seen men with degrees, piled on top of degrees, that get up and say how you and I evolved from monkeys. Maybe they did, but I sure didn't! Some of the greatest intellectual minds of the universe talk about how we evolved from a single-cell protoplasmic blob! That is beyond the comprehension of the mind. If you saw a Boeing 747 flying across the sky, wouldn't you assume that because it could fly, it can carry people, its seats are placed in rows, and that it can do all the things it can do; wouldn't you assume that somebody thought it up, and somebody put it together? Certainly you would not conclude that it was the accidental product of a tornado blowing through a junkyard. Yet the same mind can look in the sky and see a bird fly by and say, "Product of chance."

"And they exchanged the glory of the incorruptible God for an image in the form of corruptible man and of birds and four-footed animals and crawling creatures." They worshiped the creature rather than the Creator. We have the worship of the creature going on around us on a global scale. Then look what happened—here is the payoff. "Therefore God gave them over in the lust of their hearts to impurity, that their bodies might be dishonored among them. For they exchanged the truth of God for a lie, and worshiped and served the creature rather than the Creator, who is blessed forever, Amen" (Rom. 1:18–25). That is humanism! Humanism is the worship of man rather than God. That is Satan's religion, and it has been Satan's religion from the beginning. It says put your trust in man; it has become the religion of our age and of the USA.

Now look what God did. It says here that because they worshipped the creature rather than the Creator, God steps back. It is as if God has parameters or limits as to how far evil can go. He says that evil can only go so far. But God says, "If you are going to knock against those limits, and if you knock against them long enough, I am going to step back. And I will let you foul your own nest, and if you want to live like a pagan, you can." When He stepped back, what happened? There was an outbreak of sexual immorality. Does that sound familiar?

All you have to do is turn on the TV talk shows and listen to one celebrity after another brag about how they are both homosexual and heterosexual. They brag about "Yes, I have a new baby, but that baby is from the guy I was living with before, and I am now living with a different person." Today, they wear immorality as a badge of honor. We have come a long way.

> For this reason God gave them over to degrading passions; for their women exchanged the natural function for that which is unnatural, and in the same way the men abandoned that natural function of the woman and burned in their desire towards one another, men committing indecent acts and receiving

in their own person the due penalty of their error.[9]
(Rom. 1:26–27)

God says, "If you are going to live like that, I am going to step back." What happens? An outbreak of sexual immorality begins. God says, "If you are going to live like that, I am going to step back again." What happens? It culminates in an outbreak of homosexuality. People of God, we are there! We have arrived.

"And just as they did not see fit to acknowledge God any longer, God gave them over to a depraved mind, to do those things which are not proper" (Rom. 1:28). When God steps back, there is an outbreak of immorality. When we continue to push up against those limits, God will step back again, and there is an outbreak of homosexuality. When we continue to push those limits, God steps back again and turns us over to a depraved mind, to do those things that are not proper. It is a time when lawlessness begins to rule, and mankind does not have any standards by which they live by. Paul finishes the chapter by listing twenty-one signs of depravity.

> Being filled with all unrighteousness, wickedness, greed, evil; full of envy, murder, strife, deceit, malice; *they are* gossips, slanderers, haters of God, insolent, arrogant, boastful, inventors of evil, disobedient to parents, without understanding, untrustworthy, unloving, unmerciful; and although they know the

ordinance of God, that those who practice such things are worthy of death, they not only do the same, but also give hearty approval to those who practice them.[10]

In a recent (2011) UCLA study conducted by the Williams Institute, they showed that people who identify themselves as gay or lesbian represents less than 2 percent (1.7 percent to be exact) of the population in America.[11] Yet if you watch television and movies, you would think that homosexuality represents 50 percent or more of the population. God has defined marriage as between one man and one woman. If a man and a man or a woman and a woman desires to be together, that is not marriage. Marriage has been given a definition a long time ago by the One who created us male and female.

Does the Candidate Know That God Has Given to the State the Power to Execute Criminals in Instances of Murder, Kidnapping, Rape, and Treason?

"Whoever sheds man's blood, by man his blood shall be shed, for in the image of God He made man" (Gen. 9:6). Will the candidate promote capital punishment? The Bible says capital punishment is biblical. Not kind of biblical, it is very biblical. But the punishment cannot be an act of an individual; it is only acted upon by the court. The government can do it, individuals cannot. It has to be the government or the courts to authorize capital punishment. There are four areas that capital punishment was prescribed to the offender in the Bible: murder ("You shall not murder; Whoever strikes a man so that he dies shall be put to death" [Exod. 20:13, 21:12]; "But if he struck him down with an iron object, so that he died, he is a murderer. The murderer shall be put to death" [Num. 35:16]; "You shall not murder" [Deut. 5:17].), kidnapping ("Whoever steals a man and sells him, and anyone found in possession of him, shall be put to death" [Exod. 21:16].), rape ("But if in the open country a man meets a young woman who is betrothed, and the man seizes her and lies with her, then only the man who lay with her shall die" [Deut. 22:25].), and treason (Num. 16 throughout the chapter).

There are capital punishment guidelines in the Bible; one was you could not kill somebody based on one witness. You had to have two or more witnesses. "If anyone kills a person, the murderer shall be put to death at the evidence of witnesses, but no person shall be put to death on the testimony of one witness. Moreover, you shall not take ransom for the life of a murderer who is guilty of death, but he shall surely be put to death" (Num. 35:30–31). If you testify against a person that would include the death penalty and you lied as a witness, then you bear the consequences of the death penalty. So if you testify against someone and they are getting the death penalty and we find out you lied, you get the death penalty. That will make you tell the truth on the stand, because God knows that human nature will try to do evil things to hurt other people.

A second guideline was that capital punishment was public. And that is why it was a deterrent as opposed to today. Capital punishment is not a deterrent today because if everybody saw it, they would change their position. God does not play with the taking of life. Now you are messing with God; you are insulting God. What you need to know is, "I will not hold him guiltless" (Exod. 20:7), meaning those who take innocent life. You have to make the connection; the reason why crime will continue to go up is because every time God sees you messing with innocent life, His judgment will rain down on the culture that produces that. So you will see violence on the born increasing because of the violence on the unborn. If you do not make that connection, all you see is that people are wicked, and people are killing people. All you see is what people are doing, but you do not see the reason why God is allowing the violence, because we as a nation are doing the same thing privately inside of the womb.

We have mentioned Matthew earlier. "You have heard that the ancients were told, 'You shall not commit murder' And 'Whoever commits murder shall be liable to the court.' But I say to you that everyone who is angry with his brother shall be guilty before the court; And whoever says to his brother, 'You good-for-nothing,' shall be guilty before the supreme court; and whoever says, 'You fool,' shall be guilty *enough to go* into the fiery hell" (Matt. 5:21–22).

First of all, you say, "You good-for-nothing." King James uses the word *rocca*. That was an insult. It is like calling someone an idiot, and it is coming out of anger, you good-for-nothing. Men are created in the image of God, and you just said they are nothing because you are angry. What you have just done is attack God because the one you insulted in anger is made in the image of God. The worst person you know is still created in the image of God. And when out of anger you attack them, he says, "You are liable before the court."

Jesus is not talking about the earthly courts but heaven's court because this goes all the way up to heaven. What Jesus is saying, when your mouth spews malignancy that tears down another person, in the court of God, you have committed a form of murder. Based on that definition, there is not one person reading this who is not a murderer because God looks at it as attacking Him because you have attacked the image of God in another person. It is one thing to say you are acting a certain way or you are doing a certain thing, but when you attack who they are, you are attacking God. Every person bears the image of God, and anger creates the conditions for murder.

The implications of this are staggering. There are probably a lot of angry people reading this book. Psychologists tell us that one of the dominating emotions that is causing all kinds of psychotic behaviors and psychological problems is unresolved anger. You are just mad. You are mad at your dad because he left you. You are mad at your mom because she deserted you. You are mad at your brother because he didn't help you when you needed money. You are mad at your boss because he would not give you the promotion. You are mad at your mate because he/she is not loving you like you thought you should be loved and respected. And the anger spews out because you are tearing up the image of somebody else.

The problem is, when people get angry, they hurt the people that they love. They are so angry they express that anger at anybody in their space. And so, a mother is abusing their children because they are angry at the children's father. This anger is controlling you. When it controls you, you become a killer. That is what the Bible says: you become a murderer because your mouth spews an attack on God in the form of another individual. And every time you pick up the phone, it is to kill somebody. Every time you write a note, it is to kill somebody. Every time you have a word to say, it is a murderous word. He says this stems from a heart of anger. And the anger may come from legitimate pain. The worst thing about this anger is you are not committing homicide; you are committing suicide because while you have destroyed somebody else, you are destroying you, because now you have to live with this angry person, and that angry person is you.

How do I deal with this spirit of murder? Cain was upset in Genesis 4 because God did not receive his offering, and he became angry. Abel didn't do anything wrong. He was not bothering anybody, but Cain got mad at Abel because of jealousy. Now this helps me in ministry because God counseled Cain. God said, "Do not let this thing get the best of you." "Sin is crouching at the door; and its desire is for you, but you must master it" (Gen. 4:7). That helps me. I got set free when I read that. If God is counseling you and you are not listening, then I do not feel so bad if you don't listen to me. He got the best counselor available, and God could not change his mind because that is the danger with anger. It will keep you from even listening to God.

What is God's solution for dealing with your anger? Your anger is murder, remember that. It is attacking God. Here is what you have to do. It is real simple. The first thing you do with anger is forgive the person who caused it. Apart from that, you will die an angry person. You will die a murderer. You can kill all your life not physically, but you can kill emotionally: killing your kids, your relatives, and friends. Here it is. You must forgive the person who caused it. Forgiveness does not mean I forgot what happened. That is not forgiveness and is not practical. Forgive is you saying, "I will no longer relate to you based upon what has happened. I am cancelling out the debt; you do not owe me anymore." As long as somebody owes you, every time you see them, you see the bill they owe you. "You did that to me twenty-five years ago, and I have not been paid back yet. You owe me."

One of the most freeing things that I have ever done in my life was released somebody from a bill that they owed me. When I released them from the bill they owed me, I no longer related to them the same way. Now I was not expecting payment. As long as I was expecting payment when I saw them, I saw a bill. But once I release the bill, now I am not expecting the payment. So now I am free. You say, "How do I forgive them?" You tell them, "I release you for what you did to me." You call and release them so that you can stop living on the killing fields. You can stop murdering those in your vicinity.

While your emotions will have to catch up to your release you have just been set free from your prison, you say, "Okay, but what about the wrong that they did to me? How fair is that, JT?" First of all, trust me. God has let you get away with a lot of stuff. Suppose God did not let you get away with some of the things He let you get away with? Think about that. While you plot to get them back, think about what you might be getting in return. So it might make you rethink your position.

Let us suppose there is legitimate pain that you are dealing with, and that is what is causing you to become a murderer. The Bible has a simple solution for that, but it is a hard one emotionally but is the best one ever. "Vengeance is mine, says the Lord I will repay" (Heb. 10:30). I know what you are thinking you give me something practical. That sounds good, and I know what God said, but I want something to go upside that person's head tomorrow. I know what you are thinking: God is too slow because if I was God, I would have gotten them long time ago. Hit them now!

Now watch this: "Vengeance is mine I will repay, says the Lord." You either believe that or you do not. If you do not believe it, you will try to pay them back. But if you try to pay them back, then God exits the payment plan. So one of the reasons why God has not dealt with those who cause your anger is you keep getting in the way. "For the anger of man does not achieve the righteousness of God" (James 1:20). If you are in the way by running your mouth, making vengeance is yours, then vengeance is not God's. So God will let you repay. The only problem is that will not deal with your anger, and it probably will not even repay. But God says, "Vengeance is mine and I will repay."

The problem is if you have never seen God's vengeance, then you do not know what I am talking about. But there are a few people reading this who have seen what God can do when God goes upside your head. The cruelest thing you can do toward an enemy who is messing over you, the worst thing you can do to them is nothing. You just do nothing because now God can say, "You are not in My way." You have taken God off the leash, so to speak. But as long as you get in the way, God says, "I am not going after them with you. Vengeance is mine, not ours. I will repay, not we will repay. In fact, I do not even want you there when I do My thing because then you are going to start feeling sorry for them."

My point is simply this: we are all murderers. So let us get off our high horses. Also, I have no doubt when you read this and talk to others, I am going to be killed. "Did you hear the pastor talking all that crazy stuff in his book?" So I know I am going to die today. God says stop killing. Certainly, physically, but more than physically, stop killing mentally, emotionally, and spiritually. Stop killing.

God is the one who established capital punishment. Recently, two death row inmates petitioned the state of Oklahoma because of the drugs used in the lethal injections. They were claiming it was too painful to use the two-drug combination. Really? One of the men raped and killed an eleven-month-old infant. By the Old Testament standard, he would have received the death penalty for murder and rape. The other man shot his girlfriend, and when she did not die, he buried her alive. Where was all that humane treatment concern before they committed their heinous crimes against their victims? The one criminal who buried his girlfriend alive, his execution took longer than what was expected. Apparently, some of the drugs did not function properly, and his death was prolonged. His death was referred to as a "botched execution."

The Eighth Amendment reads, "Excessive bail shall not be required, nor excessive fines imposed, *nor cruel and unusual punishment inflicted*." People were saying that the execution was cruel and unusual punishment for how this convicted criminal died. A strong case could be made that the outcome was for the murderer to be dead. He ended up dead, which fulfilled the desired outcome of the state of Oklahoma. A reality is that he suffered less than his victim, who was buried alive. I would not describe the execution as a botched execution but a fulfilled desire of the state of Oklahoma.

I'm aware that a person on death row will change after being there for twenty-plus years. That does not change the fact that the crimes have been committed. I also know some innocent people have suffered by being put to death. Unfortunately, innocents always suffer at the hand of the guilty. When a pregnant mother continues to use crack during her pregnancy, the innocent child suffers drug addiction at birth. When a father commits a crime that he will be incarcerated for, his innocent family will suffer the consequences of his criminal behavior. His family will suffer significant hardship because of his actions. Please keep in mind that it was an innocent man (Jesus Christ) who was crucified for our sins that gave us redemption. Unfortunately, there will be innocent people who will suffer due to no actions on their part.

Capital punishment was given to the people of God to be a deterrent to crime and to punish the guilty. It was to be done by the state and not the individual. Even the "eye for an eye" law was administered by the state and not by the individual. It was to monitor vigilantism. God was not interested in a shootout at the OK Corral. One final observation is that the executions in the Bible were public, and this became the greatest deterrent for future criminals.

Does the Candidate Know That God Has Given the Task of Raising and Teaching Children to Parents as Opposed to the Government?

These words, which I am commanding you today, shall be on your heart. You shall teach them diligently to your sons and shall talk of them when you sit in your house and when you walk by the way and when you lie down and when you rise up. (Deut. 6:6–7)

Train up a child in the way he should go, Even when he is old he will not depart from it. (Prov. 22:6)

Fathers, do not provoke your children to anger, but bring them up in the discipline and instruction of the Lord.[12] (Eph. 6:4)

There's no easy way to say it, no soft sell here. If you don't care about your family, then you don't care about your future. Let's not try and talk about greatness in Washington because what really matters is not what happens at the White House but what is happening in your house. That is the challenge that we face. The question is, Where we are going to go to find out about family? The greatest challenge of all is what it means to be parents. To give birth to children that we then must spend approximately eighteen years molding and shaping, and twisting and turning, and fussing and causing all manner of trauma to try to raise them right.

As we look at parenting today, I want to suggest to you that if we are going to make it as parents, you need your Bible. While the schools, the government, and society have changed, children have not changed, and God has not changed. Since children have not changed, and God has not changed, we better deal with what is constant and not what is mobile.

Ephesians 6:4 reads, "Fathers, do not provoke your children to anger, but bring them up in the discipline and instruction of the Lord." Let me give you the biblical reason the father was always viewed by God as the representative head of the home. He was the one who God would speak to, and his job was to transfer to the wife and the children the word of God. He was the representative head of the home. That's why the devil wants to get rid of dads. He wants to get rid of dads so that there is no male representative at home, which places extra burden on the female. Many of you are tempted to walk out on your kids; you need to think twice. Because the Bible says he will visit the sins of the father on the children to the third and fourth generation. So when we walk out, you are not just walking out on your kids; you are walking out on your grandkids and your great-grandkids, generations down to the third and fourth generation. And if you think this generation is bad, you haven't seen anything yet. Wait until they have their kids.

I make no apology that our church will always emphasize men. Not because we are antiwomen, but we realize that in our world, we are not giving men the place of leadership. And while God has given women great gifts and great abilities that we could not function in our society without them, the great challenge for the church is to win men, to call men back to their rightful place.

Father was the logical representative of God. There is also cultural reason why he addresses fathers. In Rome, women did not have a lot of rights. They were a subjugated gender. When a baby was born in Rome, that baby would be brought to its father and placed in front of him. The father would look at their child, and if it's a thumbs-up, "I'll keep the baby," but thumbs-down, they would put the baby into the exposure and let that child die. If a man wanted his firstborn to be a boy in Rome and you brought the baby before him and it was a girl, Roman fathers, with permission of Roman law, could go thumbs down. The child would either be put in the streets to die, sold, become an orphan, or slave. The child could be raised in a brothel to become a prostitute with the full recognition of the law of the land.

But here comes Jesus. He changed the society. He says, "Fathers, you have responsibility. You are God's representatives here." Jesus says, "I know it's hard, I know you want to quit, but you can't quit because you represent God in that house. Parents, you have the right of life and death in your hands. Generations are dependent upon you, not just your kid but also their kids and their kids." You say it's too late for my kids already because my kids are older. God can still hit a bull's-eye with a crooked stick.

The first thing parents must do is encourage their children. Paul says, "Do not provoke your children to anger." That is a negative way of saying positively, "Be your child's encourager." Colossians 3:21 says, "Do not exasperate them." Don't discourage them but encourage them. One of the things that a child needs to know is that no matter what anybody else thinks about them at home, they are somebody. Many of our young people are going after significance outside of the home because they are not finding significance inside the home. They are rejected or provoked to anger.

How do you provoke or discourage a child? One way is favoritism. One way is to value one child more than another child because they have your personality or your interests. So you favor them. You remember Joseph. Jacob gave him a coat of many colors, and he provoked the other eleven brothers to wrath. And they tried to kill Joseph because his father played favorites. When it comes to your position as father and mother, you can't play favorites. Why, because they are all equally your children. The one thing about God is He plays no favorites; He's consistent. Favoritism is one way to discourage a child.

Another way to discourage a child is to try to pull them toward your dreams and you not be invested in their dreams. Don't try to make them you rather than you encouraging them to become all that God wants them to be. He says, "Don't provoke your children to anger." We discourage our children when we do not prioritize them. Why should we prioritize them? Because the family is the first responsibility. It comes before your job. If you don't accept a career move up because it would negatively impact your family, that's the decision you make. Because in the corporate world, they will tell you to sacrifice your family if you have to. They don't care about your family. They care about productivity of the company. But God says your family is first. Sometimes, parents, we will be inconvenienced to not provoke our children's wrath, where they wind up saying, "He was never there for me. You never cared for me. Your words that you love me were only words." Don't discourage your kids.

Be an example before your children, and it will encourage your children. A teacher called a father in and said, "We have a big problem with your son. He keeps stealing erasers from the classroom and takes them home." The father said,

"I don't know why he would do that. I bring home a box of erasers from work every week." The idea is to be an example that they can follow.

To be blessed meant that your father recognizes your significance and that you were the future that he was counting on you. Men, when was the last time you placed your hands on your son and you blessed him? We close our eyes and bow our heads, perhaps got down on our knees, and say, "My son, in the name of Jesus Christ of Nazareth, as a son of the living God, I bless you." If you want to impact your son, particularly one who has gone astray, because we are quick to curse (doesn't mean profanity), we are quick to say you did not do that right, why don't you change this. How come this, how come that. They have heard how bad they are, but have they ever been blessed?

There is a difference between encouragement and praise. We praise our children a lot, but we don't necessarily encourage them. Praise means that I want to be excited about what you accomplished. "You hit a home run in the baseball games, that was great. You got an *A* on your test, daughter, that was wonderful." That's praise. Praise means you did something that I want to acknowledge.

But when they are not accomplishing, they do not get praise because praise is tied to accomplishment. Encouragement is different. Encouragement is not related to what I achieve; encouragement is tied to who I am. Encouragement says, "I want to affirm you." Encouragement says, "You haven't done anything spectacular I just want to wrap my arms around you and tell you, you are my special child, that you mean a lot to me, that I love you. I passionately adore you because of who you are." When you water a drooping plant, it perks up. That's what encouragement does. Encouragement says, "I am special. I am somebody." We must encourage our children.

Secondly, if we are going to be quality parents, we must nurture our children. But bring them up. That is the same Greek word used in Ephesians 5:29 when he says, "Christ nourishes the church," which is what a husband should do to his mate. We are to nurture them. Luke 2:52 says that we are to nurture children in four areas: intellectually, spiritually, emotionally, and socially. We are to manage their development in such a way that we take responsibility for their intellectual development, physical development, and their spiritual development and for their social development. We must not only be concerned with the food they eat and the friends they play with, but also what they are learning in Sunday school and in school. In other words, those four areas of life are the four areas of nurturing.

Proverbs 22 reads, "Train up a child in the way he should go, and when he is old he would not depart from it." That is a proverb. A proverb is not a promise, but it is a truism. It is a normal way things work. "Train up a child." That word *train* means to place something up on the palate. It had to do with the way a Hebrew wife would prepare food for a little baby. They didn't have grinders like we have today. So she would take some food and put it in her mouth. She would turn it into a soft paste to place in the palette, and that would excite the baby's taste buds to eat it and swallow it.

To train meant to make something palatable in such a way that the other person who was being trained is able to digest it and benefit from it. Now when I ask you, are you training your children are you making it palatable, or are we bull dosing them, being cruel to them? The idea is to make it palatable so that it benefits them. We do more training of dogs than we do with kids.

Training is always tied to reward and punishment, not bribing and punishment. Bribing means getting you to do what I want you to do. There's a difference between reward and bribing. When he says, "Train up a child," next phrase is, "according to his way in the way he should go." When you recognize the uniqueness of each child, that means don't try to come up with a standard operation procedure for each child. Every child is different, and each one has a different temperament. So how you deal with one child may not be how you deal with another child because you must train them according to their ways, according to their unique orientation so that when they are old, they will not depart from godly training. He is not talking about old men. The word for *old* means the appearing of a beard. It meant when they were entering into adulthood. When they are older, they would not depart from it. Some of you go to church because you couldn't get away from your mother making you go the church, and now, finally, you got into church. After a while, you responded to it, and that is the concept here of nurturing.

We are to encourage our children and bring them up. Please notice parents are to raise their children. You are not to delegate the nurturing of your child to another. The church is not supposed to raise your child. The school is not supposed to raise your child. The government is not supposed to raise your child. You are supposed to raise your child because it is your child, and it is your job. We have parents today getting mad at schoolteachers because the schoolteachers didn't raise their child, or Sunday school teachers. If God wanted them to raise your child, then they would have been their child. They are your child, and your job is to raise them. That doesn't excuse people for how they impact your children, but you have the rearing responsibility. You say, "Well, I have too much on me." Well, if you cut off the TV, you will pick up a few hours right there. You are to nurture them.

Let us look at a third thing. "Bring them up in the discipline." The third thing that appears is to discipline your child. Why? Because discipline or corrective measure is proof of love. "Whom the Lord Loves He skins alive" (Heb. 12:6). Whom the Lord loves, He corrects. And it says in verse 8 that if he doesn't correct you, you are the neighbor's kids. Love is always demonstrated by discipline. If you love Johnny too much to discipline him, God says you actually hate him because love is always reflected by discipline. I know some of us think our children are little angels. You just keep waiting because as their legs get longer, their wings get shorter. Because children are born in sin, and all they need is time. Give them time to talk or to walk, and you've given time enough for them to sin. They weren't born with a spark of divinity; they were born with hell bred in them. Your job is to let them know, "You may have hell in you, but I am going to take hell out of you."

The parents' job is to challenge Satan's ownership of our children. Because they are born in sin separated from God under the curse. That's why you don't have to teach them to be selfish, to cheat, or to get an attitude or temper tantrums. How come you don't have to go to the store to get a book about how to teach my child to lie? Because it is built inside of them. They are born that way. So God has given them parents to discipline them.

But listen, children are never to be disciplined apart from love. When you discipline a child apart from love, you can do physical damage or emotional damage. If they don't know that you love them and you try to discipline them, then you can wind up hurting them physically or emotionally or inflict psychological damage because they were punished but never loved. That is why correcting your children when you are angry is not the right time. That is making you feel better but not making them do better. That's why it must be disciplined tied to love.

Proverbs is a book on parenting. Let us look at these verses and the responsibility of disciplining our children. "He who withholds his rod hates his son, but he who loves him disciplines him diligently" (Prov. 13:24). The rod was not a club. It was a spanking instrument used that would sting but do no permanent damage. It would hurt but would not abuse. He says if you don't correct them you hate him.

"Discipline your son while there is hope, and do not desire his death" (Prov. 19:18). I know some of us wish our kids were dead. He says that's not the right attitude. God said, "Don't wish he was dead. Instead, wish you were a parent, and you would correct your child. That is your responsibility."

"Foolishness is bound up in the heart of a child; the rod of discipline will remove it far from him" (Prov. 22:15). You say my child is bad. You have your rod of discipline, and that rod of discipline is designed to drive that mess out of here. We have a lot to of kids running in the street that never got disciplined at home. They never got it at home, so they are under no ones authority because they were never disciplined.

"Do not hold back discipline from the child, although you strike him with a rod, he will not die" (Prov. 23:13). He will think he is dying. He will not be dying because you are spanking life into him rather than death into him. "You

shall strike him with a rod and rescue his soul from hell."
(So you encourage him, you nurture him, and you discipline
him to save his soul from hell.) "The rod of reproof give
wisdom, but a child who gets his own way brings shame to
his mother. Correct your son and he will give you comfort;
he will also delight your soul" (Prov. 29:15, 17).

The Bible has a tragic story of a man who was a passive
father. His name is Eli. The story is found in 1 Samuel 2.
He is a preacher, but he is a passive father. It is like the
father who was on a trip. His five-year-old son said, "I want
to be in charge today."

The mother said, "Okay, you sit at the head of the table."

His older sister said, "How can you make him in charge?
He's only five years old. He has no business being in charge."

The mother said, "Just leave him alone. He's in charge."

The boy is excited and says, "I am in charge here."

The sister, wanting to embarrass him, says, "You are in
charge, you are the man in house, then how much is two
plus two?"

He looked at his sister and said, "Ask your mother."

The passive father is always saying, "Ask your mother,"
rather than consulting and making sure you have a joint
plan to deliver as head of the house. Eli was a passive father.
He was a father who overdelegated. Eli had two adult sons.
They were stealing from the church in 1 Samuel 2:14.
"Then he would thrust it into the pan, or kettle, or caldron,
or pot; all that the fork brought up the priest would take

for himself. Thus they did in Shiloh to all the Israelites who came there." They were also sleeping with the female ushers. "Now Eli was very old; and heard all that his son's were doing to all Israel, and how they lay with the women who served at the doorway of the tent of meeting" (1 Sam. 2:22).

Well, God got tired of these two kids. "For I have told him that I am about to judge his house forever for the iniquities which he knew, because his son's brought a curse on themselves and he did not rebuked them" (1 Sam. 3:13). The sons were bringing death to the house, and he did not rebuke them. What does rebuke mean? Just tell them that they are doing wrong? No. Eli told them that they were doing wrong. "No, my sons; for the report is not good which I hear the Lord's people circulating" (1 Sam. 2:24). He said, "You boys stop that. Naughty, naughty, naughty." You may say naughty, naughty to a two-year-old but not an eighteen-year-old. God said Eli did not rebuke his sons and that means followed through, not just say "no, stop that." And that's why it should be the fathers because the boys are bigger and stronger than their mother, and they lose respect, and they need a man's presence. If he is bigger than you, call your brother or an uncle or somebody else.

Discipline has to occur. What was the result? The two boys were killed. "Than the one who brought the news replied, Israel has fled before the Philistines and there has also been a great slaughter among the people, and your two sons also, Hophni and Phinehas, are dead, and the Ark of God has been taken" (1 Sam. 4:17). The nation was in trouble because the Ark of God had been taken. "It came about when he mentioned the Ark of God that Eli fell off the seat backward beside the gate, and his neck was broken and he died, for he was old and heavy. Thus he judged Israel 40 years" (1 Sam. 4:18). God took care of the father for his lack of parental involvement as well. "Now, his daughter-in-law, Phinehas' wife, was pregnant and about to give birth; and when she heard the news that the Ark of God was taken and her father-in-law and her husband had died, she kneeled down and gave birth, for her pains came upon her. And about the time of her death the women, who stood by her said to her, 'Do not be afraid, for you have given birth to a son.' But she did not answer or pay attention." (So she dies as well after giving birth to a son.) "And she called the boy Ichabod, saying, 'The glory has departed from Israel.'" That is what is happening in America: the glory of the Lord is on its way out. Because the families have decided to let the parents obey the children, we have madness out there in the name of freedom because we have failed to maintain the stability of the parents.

Fourthly, instruct them in the Lord. Being supported by their wives gives your children a biblical education. Make sure they are gaining a spiritual-based education in the Lord. In Deuteronomy 6:2, he says, "Teach them My commandments so that you and your son and your grandson might fear the Lord your God, to keep all His statues and His commandments which I command you, all the days of your life, and that your days may be prolonged."

We get . upset because they've taken the Ten Commandments out of the schools and out of the government. I want to know, are they in your home? God never told your kid's teacher to teach them the Ten Commandments. God is concerned about what you are doing in your home. You are to pass unto your children and your grandchildren the Word of God. If you don't take the time to review sermons and lessons with your family, have prayer with your children, then don't blame the government, the school, or the streets for your messed up kids. That becomes the parents' responsibility.

In verse 4, we are to teach them "that there's only one God." In verse 5, there's only one love. "You shall love the Lord your God with all your heart and with all your soul and with all your might." Then in verse 6, "There is only one law the law I am giving you." So when they come and tell you, "But Johnny's mother…" Well, when you start living in Johnny's house, we can discuss that. But your mother and I have a biblical approach. That doesn't mean you don't listen to them. You want to listen to them and instruct them in the Lord.

Teach them convincingly in verse 6, "They must be on your heart." "You shall teach them diligently to your sons and shall talk to them when you sit in your house and [teach them conversationally] when you walk by the way and when you lie down and when you rise up." It doesn't have to be a formal Bible study. Do it as you are watching TV, going to school, playing, and sitting down to dinner. You are to use every opportunity available to you to teach your children. You are to teach them creatively. "You shall bind them as a sign on your hand and they shall be as frontals on your forehead" (Deut. 6:8). Make memory verses out of them. And finally, do it conspicuously. Growing up as a child, while we had our meals, our parents taught us to recite a Bible passage before we ate. That has been of great benefit to me because I have many verses committed to memory. My baby brother would almost always quote, "Jesus wept." I guess he was ready to eat. "You shall write them on the doorpost of your house and on your gate" (Deut. 6:9). In other words, make it obvious.

Parents are responsible for their children led by the fathers. Now some of you your children are half-grown, and you say I was working too much, I have failed, I was building my business. What do I do? Psalms 127:4 says, "That children of a man are like arrows." If you shot crooked and you missed the target many years ago, you feel like a failure; you have already launched your arrows. Then you get on your knees, and you pray for a good wind. God has got to catch that errant arrow and steer it back on target. There's one thing left you can do: get on your knees for that wayward child for those failed years. You say,

"God, catch them and steer them back the right way." You can go to prayer for your kids. You know why? Because even if you have missed the target as a parent, there's still a Heavenly Father who can catch that wayward arrow and bring it home.

Please note there is nowhere that says the church is responsible for raising your children, the government is responsible for raising your children, the school system is responsible for raising your children, or even the daycare is responsible for raising your children. YOU ARE RESPONSIBLE FOR RAISING YOUR CHILDREN!

Does the educational philosophy of the candidate empower the parents or the government teachers' unions to raise your children? I believe the parents have a choice on where they send their children for an education. If the view of the candidate is the belief that the government is responsible for raising your children, then you will see less freedom for parents and further government intrusion.

Does the Candidate Know That God Commands Believers to Preach the Gospel to Every Creature?

America was founded on godly principles, and there is no doubt about that. The tragedy is we are losing our heritage. The Supreme Court made rulings in the early '60s that eliminated Bible readings and prayer from public places such as schools. In the '80s, the Supreme Court ruled that you could not hang posted copies of the Ten Commandments on the walls of our schools because students might read them and obey them. These decisions are contrary to the founding of our country. As a believer in the saving grace of Jesus Christ, it is obvious that our Supreme Court is actually fighting against God. I will let you in on a little secret: I read the back of the book, and we win, and the United States Supreme Court will lose.

We have been given commands in the New Testament to take the message of Jesus Christ to the nations, to all peoples everywhere. Take a look at the words of Jesus:

> And He said to them, "Go into all the world and preach the gospel to all creation. (Mark 16:15)

> And Jesus came up and spoke to them, saying, "All authority has been given to Me in heaven and on earth. Go therefore and make disciples of all the nations, baptizing them in the name of the Father and the Son and the Holy Spirit, teaching them to observe all that I commanded you; and lo, I am with you always, even to the end of the age."[13] (Matt. 28:18–20)

These passages are in the imperative mode. That means they are a command and are not optional. There are five purposes that the Bible has called all Christians to do. Those purposes are worship, fellowship, discipleship, ministry, and evangelism. All of us are called to do all of the purposes, but there is one of these that we cannot do in eternity. The one that is limited to our time on earth is evangelism. When we get into eternity, all that will be present will be believers. There will be no need to evangelize anyone. Thus, God has called all Christians to make it their mission to share the good news.

So my question is, Will the candidate use government to restrict Christianity in public places, schools, as well as over the airwaves and on the Internet, or will he allow the Gospel to be advanced? Will the candidate not discriminate against Christianity and treat it with a level playing field as other religious beliefs?

If you are Jewish or Christian, then your faith is allowed to be made fun of and denigrated. Yet it appears that other faiths do not get the same treatment in America. Efforts are made in schools to have teaching on Islam. The students are encouraged to wear Muslim clothing and to write a prayer to Allah under the guise of teaching religious tolerance. Yet the same school will not allow a Christmas tree or Nativity scene in that same classroom. How is that religious tolerance? Could we be more intolerant?

Jesus said in John 14:6, "I am the way, and the truth, and the life. No one comes to the Father except through Me." No one means no one. That might seem narrow-minded; however, since God created us, He has the right to set the guidelines on how we get to Him. Plus, Jesus died for the sins of mankind. Do not underestimate that act. It is hard for us to think about eternity. We do better with eternity in the future because it includes us. We have a harder time with eternity in the past.

When Jesus was on the cross, suspended between heaven and earth, He cried out, "My God, My God! Why have You forsaken Me?" For the first and only time in the existence of God the Son (Jesus Christ), He was separated from God the Father and God the Holy Spirit. Jesus was separated not because He did something wrong but because I did something wrong. At that moment, when Jesus cried out, He had *all* of my sins upon His shoulders. My sins are enough to weigh anyone down, but He not only had my sins He had all the sins of everyone on the face of the earth that had lived up to that time, that was living at that time, and that will live in the future.

God is a holy God, and His holiness demands that He deals with sin. God did not give us a pass on our sin; someone died in our stead. That is what the cross is about. The good news is that on the cross, Jesus took my sins and nailed them to the cross. Look at Colossians 2:9–15:

> For in Him all the fullness of Deity dwells in bodily form, and in Him you have been made complete, and He is the head over all rule and authority; and in Him you were also circumcised with a circumcision made without hands, in the removal of the body of the flesh by the circumcision of Christ; having been buried with Him in baptism, in which you were also raised up with Him through faith in the working of God,

who raised Him from the dead. When you were dead in your transgressions and the uncircumcision of your flesh, He made you alive together with Him, having forgiven us all our transgressions, having canceled out the certificate of debt consisting of decrees against us, which was hostile to us; and He has taken it out of the way, having nailed it to the cross. When He had disarmed the rulers and authorities, He made a public display of them, having triumphed over them through Him.[14]

Paul paints the picture that when Jesus was on the cross, He cancelled out the certificate of debt against us. When the Romans crucified a person, they would have all His charges read off in a decree. They would then take those decrees and place them over the head of the person crucified. That way, everyone would know what they were guilty of doing. What this shows us is when Christ was crucified, Satan came with a list of all of my sins—and the truth be told, that was just an index of my sins—and said, "James Taylor is guilty of all of these sins." Jesus then agrees with Satan and says, "You are correct. James is guilty of all these sins, and I see you missed a few." But the grace of God is that Jesus takes the paper, with the list of my sins, and takes His blood and washes the paper with it and then hands it back to Satan. When Satan receives it, he is handed a blank sheet of paper because Jesus nailed them to the cross.

That is what is meant by disarming the rulers and authorities. Jesus made a public spectacle of Satan and his demonic horde because all the evidence against me miraculously disappeared. That is the grace of God. That is why what Jesus did on the cross is so important. That is why Jesus said in John 14:6, "I am the way, and the truth, and the life. No one comes to the Father except through Me." If we could get to the Father any other way, then the death and resurrection of Jesus was in vain. Jesus didn't separate Himself from God the Father and God the Holy Spirit just because He was having a bad day. Jesus tasted what hell will be like on the cross, for hell is nothing more than the absence of the presence of God. Jesus experienced hell on the cross for all of us so we do not have to experience hell. That is why we are called to evangelize our world. Again, it is in the imperative mode, a command and not an option.

We do not have to jam the Bible down the throat of anyone. Our lives are to be a message of Jesus Christ. We are to be Jesus with flesh so others can see Jesus in us. On the back of my business card are these words: "If we meet and you forget me, you have lost nothing. But if you meet Jesus Christ and forget Him, you have lost everything." That is a message of truth that is not jammed down someone's throat. They can get the message.

On my cell phone I leave the message, "You have reached JT. I am unavailable at this time, but I do have a message for you. Did you know that God loves you so much that He sent His only Son to die for your sins? Now…if you got better news than that, then go ahead and leave a message." Usually they hang up; however, I do receive many, "Well, I don't have better news, but I'm going to leave a message anyway." That is letting them know that Jesus is the answer to life's issues. You don't have to jam God's Word down someone's throat.

Whenever I go to a restaurant and the server takes my order, I always ask them a question. I say to them, "When our meal arrives, we are going to be asking God's blessing on our meal. Is there anything we can be asking God to bless you with while we are praying?" I cannot tell you how many opportunities for ministry this has provided. Again, this is not shoving a Bible down someone's throat; it is caring about another person. Someone once said, "People don't care how much you know until they see how much you care." That is what the Gospel message is all about. It is about being in an intimate relationship with God. You can do all of those things to touch someone's life.

This is why a candidate needs to be willing to allow the Gospel to be preached; it has eternal consequences. Without the truth of knowing Jesus Christ, no man will spend eternity in the presence of God. A little side note: if, in the future, our Supreme Court rules that we cannot preach the gospel, then I will have a new prison ministry.

Does the Candidate Know That God Supports the Right to Bear Arms?

When Christ sent out the seventy, He told them not to take anything with them. They were to be taken care of by the people they ministered to. Luke and Matthew record the account.

> And He said to them, "Take nothing for *your* journey, neither a staff, nor a bag, nor bread, nor money; and do not *even* have two tunics apiece. Whatever house you enter stay there until you leave that city. And as for those who do not receive you, as you go out from that city, shake the dust off your feet as a testimony against them." (Luke 9:3–5)

> "And as you go, preach, saying, 'The kingdom of heaven is at hand.' Heal *the* sick, raise *the* dead, cleanse *the* lepers, cast out demons. Freely you received, freely give. Do not acquire gold, or silver, or copper for your money belts, or a bag for *your* journey, or even two coats, or sandals, or a staff; for the worker is worthy of his support.[15] (Matt. 10:7–10)

However, when Christ was sending out His disciples into the hostile world from the Upper Room, right before He was to be crucified, He said, "And He said to them, 'But now, whoever has a money belt is to take it along, likewise also a bag, and whoever has no sword is to sell his coat and buy one…'They said, 'Lord, look, here are two swords.'

And He said to them, 'It is enough'" (Luke 22:36, 38). In so doing, Christ provided not only for the self-defense of His disciples but also their right to defend themselves from aggression—this would be the equivalent of our modern day Second Amendment rights. Jesus was saying to all of us that we have the right to bear arms.

His disciples took this command very seriously. You will recall that when Jesus was in the garden of Gethsemane and the high priests sent the soldiers to arrest Him, Peter took Christ literally. Peter pulled out his sword and cut off the ear of the high priest's servant. "Simon Peter then, having a sword, drew it and struck the high priest's slave, and cut off his right ear; and the slave's name was Malchus. So Jesus said to Peter, "Put the sword into the sheath; the cup which the Father has given Me, shall I not drink it?" (John 18:10–11).

The cities in America with the most restrictive gun laws are the cities that have some of the highest gun violence in the country. According to the Second Amendment, a well-regulated militia is necessary to make sure that the state stays free. In my great state of Oklahoma, we have an open carry law. However, that does not stop people from trying to introduce legislation to try to restrict those freedoms.

One of the primary reasons why the National Rifle Association got started was to train and arm blacks so that they could defend themselves against the Ku Klux Klan. We do not need more restrictions on our right to bear arms.

Even Jesus recognized a need for one to be able to defend themselves from aggressors. The Second Amendment says, "Shall not be infringed." There are way too many gun laws already infringing upon our right to bear arms.

Therefore, a good question for any candidate is whether he believes in the Second Amendment to the constitution guarantees an individual right to bear arms. The Second Amendment reads, "A well-regulated militia, being necessary to the security of a free State, the right of the people to keep and bear arms, shall not be infringed." Does the candidate support endless regulations and licensing requirements upon firearms, thus paving the way toward their ultimate and total governmental confiscation? If our Second Amendment right is taken away from us, we will lose all of our other rights as well. The Second Amendment is the linchpin of our freedoms. No right to bear arms, and it is only a matter of time before all our freedoms are stripped from us.

Does the Candidate Know That the Bible Teaches That All People Have Equal Dignity and Worth?

There is no place for racism, prejudice, and discrimination in the body of Christ. "There is neither Jew nor Greek, there is neither slave nor free man, there is neither male nor female; for you are all one in Christ Jesus" (Gal. 3:28).

Will the candidate enforce all of our laws equally and fairly among all people regardless of gender, ethnicity, and socio-economic status? "Differing weights are an abomination to the LORD, and a false scale is not good" (Prov. 20:23). Discrimination against racial minorities should no more be tolerated than reverse discrimination against whites through quotas. White aggression against racial minorities should be punished to the full extent of the law and so should Black Panther voter intimidation.

One of the reasons we have not had revival in America in years is because the church of Jesus Christ has continually been split up with racism, prejudice, and discrimination. We have refused to be the one people of God. And God does not work through disunity. The Bible says that "Satan is a roaring lion seeking whom he may devour." But many Christians don't know when a lion roars. Lions don't roar before they kill their prey. They roar after they have killed their pray because lions are terrified of jackals. Jackals travel in packs of five and ten at a time. They have razor-like teeth and lightning speed. A lion, in order to scare the jackals away, will send out a loud roar. And the jackals, being intimidated, won't come and pick up the carcass of the deer that the lion has killed. In other words, the lion rules by intimidation.

But if those jackals only knew that all they had to do was show up. If they just kept on coming in spite of that loud noise, in spite of that ferocious roar, the lion would gladly give up the deer because he isn't crazy. He knows he can't handle ten jackals.

Satan has got a big mouth, but if God's people would ever just get together and keep on coming, Satan will give up our cities, our communities, and our families because he knows he can't handle the *one, united* church of Jesus Christ. It's time we come together. That means that when you read this, I must be your brother. I don't want you to talk about it, I want you to walk about it. If your biological brother does not know Jesus, then I should be closer to you than your brother in the flesh. Because when your brother in the flesh dies, you will never see him again. But when we are translated to glory, we are going to be a family for eternity.

It is like the story of the Lone Ranger. He was going across the northern plains, and when he reached the northern rim, a group of Native Americans were on the warpath. Tonto said, "Kimosabe, what we do now?"

The Lone Ranger said, "Well, I guess we go south."

When they got to the southern rim, another group of Native Americans are on the warpath. Tonto said, "Kimosabe, what we do now?"

Lone Ranger said, "Well, I guess we got to go east."

They head to the eastern rim, and another group of Native Americans are on the warpath. "What we do not, Kimosabe," asked Tonto?

"Well, I guess we have to go west. It is the only way left." Another group of Native Americans were on the warpath.

This time, the Lone Ranger asked the question, "Tonto, what we do now?"

Tonto says, "What you mean 'we,' Pale Face?"

Don't call me Kimosabe in private and then not know me in public. Don't call me brother in church and then don't know me when we are in a different environment. If I am good enough to be your brother in a church building, then I am good enough to be your brother living next door to you, going to church with you, riding in the same car as you. I'm good enough to be your brother all the time, not just some of the time. And that is what we need today. We need a group of people who are brothers all the time. John 17 says, "That they may be one." The world needs us. Our world is falling apart, and it needs leadership. And that leadership won't come from politics. Most whites are Republican because of your moral concerns. Most blacks are Democrats because of your social concerns. I'm here to tell you, God doesn't ride the back of donkeys or elephants. He doesn't care what you are.

Do you remember in Joshua 5, Joshua was going out to battle, and he saw a huge man that was captain of a large army. Joshua asked him, "Whose side are you on? Are you on our side? Because if you are on our side, we have a better chance of winning. But if you are on their side, I'm going to have to rethink my battle strategy." The man said, "You are thoroughly confused. I am neither on your side, nor am I on their side. I am captain of the Lord's army. I did not come to take sides. I come to take over." God has come to take over. That means that we must be the one people of God.

In the Bible, we have a brotherhood problem. One day, Peter was having devotions on his rooftop, and God let him see a sheet come down from heaven with all manner of animals on it. Peter had been kosher, but God tells him he can now eat anything, for Peter has always wanted to know what it tastes like to have some chitterlings, hog mauls, and pork chops. He never had the opportunity to eat that. So in Galatians 2, we find him eating at the Soul Shack with the Gentiles. It says that he was having a good ole time, sucking on neck bones, eating pig's feet, and slurping down those chitterlings. He was just having a good ole hog-eating time.

While he and some of his friends were eating, some boys from the hood showed up. The Bible says some Jews from Antioch sent by James showed up and got ticked off that their Jewish brother had the audacity to sit down and actually socialize with the hated Gentiles. "Peter, follow me now." Peter, being intimidated by his same-race Jewish brothers, backed up from the table, got up, and left. It says that when Peter got up and left, the rest of the Jews with him left. Because, you see, Peter is the leader, and a mist in the pulpit is a fog in the pew! When the leaders aren't right, when pastors won't preach on racism, when pastors skip James 2, when churches won't deal with racism, when fathers who are supposed to be leaders won't teach their children about the evil of racism, how else do you expect there not to be another generation that is more racist than the generation before it?

The Bible says that not only did Peter get up, but Barnabas got up too. Oh no! Not my boy, Barney. Anybody but Barnabas. Why, because Barnabas was raised in Cyprus. He was raised with Gentiles, grew up with Gentiles, and went to school with Gentiles. But he was so intimidated by his Jewish pastor and his Jewish friends that he got up and left the Gentiles hanging. And they would have gotten away with it except for one thing: Paul showed up for some neck bones too!

In Galatians 2, Paul said in verse 11, "When I saw what they did." In verse 14, "When I saw them compromise the truth of the Gospel." When he saw that they were preaching one thing in their church but living another way, he did not hold a seminar. He did not hold a racial reconciliation meeting. He said, "I condemned them in public on the spot, because if you are going to act a fool in public, I'm going to straighten you out in public."

> But when Cephas came to Antioch, I opposed him to his face, because he stood condemned. For prior to the coming of certain men from James, he used to eat with the Gentiles; but when they came, he *began* to withdraw and hold himself aloof, fearing the party of the circumcision. The rest of the Jews joined him in hypocrisy, with the result that even Barnabas was carried away by their hypocrisy. But when I saw that

they were not straightforward about the truth of the gospel, I said to Cephas in the presence of all, "If you, being a Jew, live like the Gentiles and not like the Jews, how *is it that* you compel the Gentiles to live like Jews?"[16]

People of God, it doesn't take four hundred years to fix racism. It takes four minutes when you have the truth. And we have the truth; we have the Word of God. The truth must come before your race, must come before your class, and must come before your culture. It must be the truth all the time first. What we want to do is excuse people's racism and give them fifty lifetimes to fix it while our world is going to hell in a handbasket rather than say, "Fix your racism, and we will work with your feelings along the way." We need people who will go to the wall on this issue.

You say, "Wait a minute. Peter was born a Jew, he was developed a Jew. How do you expect him to overcome what his mother and daddy ingrained in him?" Listen, when you committed your life to Jesus Christ, your belief system changed and became conformed to the image of Christ. Jesus said, "Unless you hate your mother and hate your father, and hate your sister and hate your brother, and yes, even hate yourself, you cannot be my disciples." Your family must come second to Jesus Christ, not first. So if you were raised wrong, then you start correcting your family. But you do not operate out of a racist mentality and expect God to do something in racially torn America. It is time for

Christians to stand up and say, "I'm not ashamed. I don't mind being identified with you. We have the truth!"

Don't misunderstand me. I am not suggesting that God wants all of us to be monolithic. He doesn't want all of us to be the same. You must understand. There has got to be a standard! God is not asking you to like soul music, and He didn't asking me to like country and western, thank God! But what he is doing is demanding that whether you are black, white, Hispanic, or Asian, that you are Christian first!

In fact, it is wrong to call yourself a black Christian or a white Christian or a Hispanic Christian or an Asian Christian. When you do that, you make black, white, Asian, Hispanic an adjective and Christian a noun. And it is the job of the adjective to modify the noun. So you have to keep changing the noun *Christian* to make it look like whatever color adjective you give it. Christianity must always be in the adjectival position, and your color should always be in the noun position. Because if anything changes, it's the noun of your humanity and not the adjective of your faith! We have always got to be Christians first!

The only group that can bring our culture and chaos back together is Christians. When the nations tried to get together at the tower of Babel, God dispersed them. Why, because God never wanted there to be social unity without spiritual unity. So how in the world can there be social unity out there in the world, unless there is spiritual unity in the body of Christ. But there was one time when there was unity in the Bible, on the day of Pentecost. People from Asia, Africa, and the Middle East all came together on the day of Pentecost. Why, because the fullness of the Spirit had come. You always know when God is at work because there is room for everybody at the cross.

So what does that mean? It means we got to get busy. It means we have to stop talking it and start walking it. First of all, *individually*. After reading this, you must have the commitment that says, "I am going to build a personal intimate relationship with a brother of a different race over the course of this next year. I am going to build a bond. I am going to commit myself to another brother, who loves my same Lord, who is of a different race. As long as he is following Christ, then we are going to walk together.

No more excuses. No more "I don't know any black people, or I don't know any white people." Just look around you. Look on the job, look down the street. And if you have to drive across town, then drive across town. Go out of your way to say, "I am going to build a relationship." "If someone says, 'I love God,' And hates his brother, he is a liar; for the one who does not love his brother whom he has seen, cannot love God whom he has not seen" (1 John 4:20). You must take the risk to build relationships.

Then, as a *family*. We have racist kids because we have racist parents. Expose your children to people of a different race. Invite them over for dinner, go to a ball game, and interact with them. Decide that my family is going to be exposed to the multicultural environment in which we live. We have a generation of families that have no dads. Some of you men need to decide to become a surrogate father to a boy that doesn't have a dad. And when we go to a ball game, he goes to a ball game. And when we go for ice cream, he goes for ice cream. Guess what? Your kids are going to grow up knowing that there is a world bigger than the world they grew up in.

Then, as *churches*. That is the answer. Everybody is saying the government ought to get out of welfare. I agree 100 percent; welfare was never meant to be the mission of the state in the Bible. But listen to me. You can't beat something with nothing. You just can't say, "Government get out," if the church hasn't prepared itself to come in. If the president said, "Look, since you Christians are talking, what are we going to do?" January 1, we are going to abolish welfare. We wouldn't be ready for that because we can complain, but we have not set up anything to fix it. If black and white churches and all the colors in between decided to be the people of God, we could make sure that there were no families, particularly a Christian family, who had to be on welfare anymore.

Because if the church was being the church, then a black church in the inner city would partner up with a white church in the suburb. The black church would provide job skills and GED training. And the white church would provide job opportunities and exposure. And people would be getting jobs, boys would be getting dads, people would be gaining skills all in the name of Jesus Christ. That's what the church can do. If the church is going to make a difference in the twenty-first century, we need to understand that we need to minister to the whole person. I know that many of you are anti-abortion. I am too. But that is only a part of the story. God's not only concerned about the fetus in the womb. He's concerned about the life to the tomb. He's concerned about cradle to grave, pillar to post, womb to tomb. Let's come up with a whole life ministry involving all Christians to demonstrate what the church of Jesus Christ can do to transform our cities.

Then, in our *society*. We need to serve notice to our society. We need Christians who are going to go public and let our society know that my God has a multicolor coalition that I am a part of, and I'm not ashamed! It is time for us to go public. It's time for us to come out of the closet. Everybody else has come out of the closet; it's time for Christians to come out too.

A man was visiting a sanitarium. He saw many insane people out on a field. When he saw them, he said to himself, "There is only one guard, one gate, and five hundred inmates, whose elevators don't go all the way to the top. Why don't they escape?" He went over to the guard and asked him, "Aren't you afraid?"

The guard said, "No, I'm not afraid."

The man continued, "Aren't you scared they are going to get together and break out of here?"

The guard responded, "No, I am not afraid."

The man asked, "Why?"

The guard replied, "Simple, lunatics don't unite."

We, the body of Christ, have got to be crazy not to get together as Christians in light of what's happening in our world. Only crazy people don't get together. We have got to be crazy to have the power of God in us and not get together to end racism.

Our society desperately needs the body of Christ to come together. The question I have is, When will we unite? I consider the Lord's Prayer to be John 17 when Jesus was praying in the garden of Gethsemane. We know that His prayer was so intense that His sweat was like great drops of blood. "And being in agony He was praying very fervently; and His sweat became like drops of blood, falling down upon the ground" (Luke 22:44). During this prayer is when he asked God to come up with another way to deliver Him. But Jesus said, "Not My will but Your will be done." But in this passage in John 17, Jesus prayed twice that we might be one. In other words, that the body of Christ might come together regardless of race, creed, color, and be the one true body of Christ. Billy Graham once said that the eleven o'clock worship hour is the most segregated hour in America. The great tragedy is that he is so right about that. We have got to be crazy to not come together as one united body of Christ.

5

Christians Are to Vote
on Foreign Affairs Issues

Does the Candidate Know
That the Concept of the Individual Nation States
Originated with God?

"And He made from one man [the literal translation is "one blood"] every nation of mankind to live on all the face of the earth [This means that we all can trace our origin back to Adam.], having determined their appointed times and the boundaries of their habitation" (Acts 17:26). Nations have been established by God. In fact, we are told that not only does God establish nations, but He has determined their boundaries and how long they will be in existence. Will the candidate favor submitting our political sovereignty to an unaccountable transnational organization (the United Nations) all in the name of global governance? Since God has established national entities and their existing borders, will the candidate enforce our borders, or will he leave America vulnerable to terrorist attacks through a porous border policy? The United Nations does not have America's sovereignty as a top priority. Our sovereignty, as well as any nations, comes from God and not the United Nations.

> At one moment I might speak concerning a nation or concerning a kingdom to uproot, to pull down, or to destroy *it;* if that nation against which I have spoken turns from its evil, I will relent concerning the calamity I planned to bring on it. Or at another moment I might speak concerning a nation or concerning a kingdom to build up or to plant *it;* if it does evil in My sight by not obeying My voice, then I will think better of the good with which I had promised to bless it.[1] (Jer. 18:7–10)

Notice the principles we can glean from the Jeremiah and Acts passages of Scripture. From the book of Acts, we see that all mankind come from one blood or person. In the book of Genesis, God gave man dominion over the earth, not over other men. God determines the boundary of all nations and how long they exist. Not only does He do that, but God is the one who places leaders in position, and He is the one who removes leaders. When King Nebuchadnezzar had a dream, he went to the wise men of his day to get an interpretation to the dream. The king decided that if they were truly wise men, then they would be able to tell the king the dream and the interpretation. They were unable to do either, and the king issued a decree to kill all the wise men as imposters. God gave Daniel the dream and the interpretation.

> Then the mystery was revealed to Daniel in a night vision. Then Daniel blessed the God of heaven; Daniel said, "Let the name of God be blessed forever and ever, For wisdom and power belong to Him. It is He who changes the times and the epochs; He removes kings and establishes kings; He gives wisdom to wise men And knowledge to men of understanding. It is He who reveals the profound and hidden things; He knows what is in the darkness, And the light dwells with Him. To You, O God of my fathers, I give thanks and praise, For You have given me wisdom and power; Even now You have made known to me what we requested of You, For You have made known to us the king's matter."[2] (Dan. 2:19–23)

Daniel makes it clear that it is God who is responsible for who leads a country. When we look at the Jeremiah passage, we find that God may decide to destroy a nation and remove them off the earth because of their sin and rebellion. However, if that nation decides to repent, then God may relent and allow the nation to remain longer. Regardless of if God allows the nation to remain longer or if He removes the nation from His sight, it is all God's decision.

Our Founding Fathers knew that at times a nation can violate God's Word and that there would be consequences for those violations. We have talked about that in the beginning of this book that the framers asked themselves how God punished a nation for violating God's law. They felt that God would use nature to punish the nation. That means hurricanes, tornadoes, earthquakes, floods, snowstorms, and any other natural occurrences of nature. Almost universally, whether liberal or conservative, people say that it's bad theology to say natural disasters are a judgment of God. Almost no one today believes God singles out individuals or groups for special punishment in their lifetimes. God doesn't work like that is what we are told.

Romans 1:18 states that "The wrath of God is revealed from heaven against all ungodliness and unrighteousness of men, who suppress the truth in unrighteousness." To say that God never visits individuals or groups of people with divine judgment for sin is false. Margaret Clarkson writes,

> It is important to distinguish between suffering as judgment for sin and suffering as the consequences of sin. Implicating God's judgment against sin in general is the simple law of cause and effect: sin gives rise to consequences for those who indulge in it. Just as it is with the [penal] laws of our country, if we transgress against God's natural, moral or spiritual laws, we will suffer the inevitable consequences. God's judgment is

set against sin itself rather than the sinner. If we sin willfully and persistently, we invite the consequences that must follow sin, and this will involve suffering.[3]

The Scriptures do teach that it is possible to suffer either God's direct punishment for sin or sins unavoidable consequences. When the wrath of God falls, people suffer the natural result. That is why the Apostle Paul recorded these words in Galatians 6:7: "Do not be deceived, God is not mocked; for whatever a man sows this he will also reap." The real question becomes, "Does God judge sin?" The biblical answer is yes! George Mason, on the convention floor, gave several biblical examples of how God did punish sin. Our Founding Fathers would have answered this question with a resounding "yes."

We need to realize that God deals with sin. Depending upon the severity of the sin, divine judgment may be complete and irreversible (e.g., Noah's flood, the destruction of Sodom and Gomorrah; Gen. 6 and 19), or it may be partial and remedial (e.g., Jonah's warning to Nineveh, the Babylonian captivity). Just as the family is a unit wherein the whole suffers for the sins of one member, society is also a unit, and the consequences are the same. Realize that when God sends judgment, His mercy is also in operation. When God sent Jonah to preach to the Ninevites to repent or else judgment would be the outcome, they repented. When they did, God spared them. His mercy and grace was in effect.

It is not politically correct to suggest that God judges sin; nevertheless, our Founding Fathers were not concerned about being politically correct. They were more concerned that this nation operated on moral principles based on the Bible and, even more specifically, the Gospel of Jesus Christ. Despite the fact that my view is apparently in the minority, it still does not change the validity of my position. If our Founding Fathers were correct in their assumption that God punishes national sin with national calamity, then we should see other evidences of this principle.

George Washington in his Farewell Address said, "Reason and experience both forbid us to expect that national morality can prevail in exclusion of religious principles." He tied our stability as a nation to our religious and moral lives. Would you describe us as a nation that practices high morality? Would you say that our elected leaders represent high moral standards? There are consequences when a nation's leaders and that nation's people sin (break the laws of God).

The best example of this is the nation of Israel. God had warned them about being obedient to Him and doing all that was written in the law as part of their preservation as a nation. They violated this principle, among other things, and Israel was scattered to the four corners of the earth. God also determined that He would regather them as a nation from the four corners of the earth. The regathering of Israel as a nation is one of the most amazing demonstration of the hand of God in world history. The point is simply that God establishes national boundaries, how long those boundaries will be in existence, who and how long the leader will be in power. It is not a decision of man; it is not the United Nations' role to determine the things of God.

Does the Candidate Know That God Promises to Bless Those Who Bless Israel and to Curse Those Who Curse Israel?

"And I will bless those who bless you, and the one who curses you I will curse. And in you all the families of the earth will be blessed" (Gen. 12:3). Therefore, another important question is, Will the candidate favor reducing Israel's existing borders in exchange for the illusion of peace, making Israel vulnerable to attack by her hostile neighbors? Those who are encouraging Israel to return to the 1967 borders obviously have not been to Israel to see that is an asinine suggestion. There is no way that Israel could defend themselves from neighbors who publicly declare their intent on annihilating Israel off the face of the earth. Satan's ambition is to eradicate the Jewish people and State of Israel off the face of the earth (Rev. 12:1, 13–17; Gen. 37:9–10). A candidate's view on Israel tells me whether he is cooperating with God's agenda or with Satan's agenda.

We are going to take some time here to look at Israel's past, present, and future. For two thousand years, the official position of Christianity has been that in 70 AD. God poured out His wrath upon the Jews, set them aside, and has no further purpose for them. Modern Christianity believes that the Jews are Christ killers, and therefore, the Jews are to be persecuted, and they have been. Romans 9–11 says that is a lie, that God still loves the Jews and has a purpose for them, and God is going to bring a remnant of the Jews, one-third of them, to salvation in Christ. You must understand a little bit of Israel's history to fully appreciate God's statement of blessings and curses for how one treats the nation of Israel. This is not an insignificant statement.

The prophecies concerning Israel are placed into three categories. The first are the prophecies that have already been fulfilled. The second are the prophecies being fulfilled right now. The third are the prophecies that are yet to be fulfilled. God is a sovereign God and knows the end from the beginning. In the mind of God, the future events are a certainty despite what we might believe.

Prophecies Already Fulfilled

Number one and two are the dispersion and the persecution of the Jewish people. In the Old Testament, we are told that a time will come when God will disperse the Jewish people to the four corners of the earth. In the city of Jerusalem, there is a place called Yad Vashem. It is the museum of the Holocaust. In Yad Vashem, you can see the gold bricks made from the gold extracted from the teeth of the Jews. You will view lampshades made out of human skin. And you will find the clothing of babies that were sent to the incinerators. You cannot begin to imagine the atrocities that were committed by Hitler. During that time, the Jews were afraid to sleep at night because it was at nighttime when the Germans would come to take them to be killed. Then the Germans changed it to the daytime that the Jews would be taken to be killed. The Jews lived in dread and fear for their very lives constantly.

> Moreover the Lord will scatter you among all the peoples, from one end of the earth to the other end of the earth; and there you shall serve other gods, wood and stone, which you and your fathers have not known. And among those nations you shall find no rest, and there shall be no resting place for the soul of your foot; but there the Lord will give you a trembling heart, failing of eyes, and despair of soul. So your life shall hang in doubt before you; and you shall be in dread night and day, and shall have no assurance of your life. In the morning you shall say, "Would that it were evening!" And at evening you shall say, "Would that it were morning!" Because of the dread of your heart which you dread, and the sight of your eyes which you shall see.[4] (Deut. 28:64–67)

That has been the plight of the Jewish people for almost two thousand years as they have wandered around the earth. They have been persecuted almost everywhere they went. There are Latin American Jews, African Jews, Asian Jews, Russian Jews, and American Jews, and Canadian Jews. There are Jewish people in almost every country of the world.

The third prophecy is desolation. God promised that after their dispersion, their land would become desolate, and their cities would become waste (Lev. 26:33). Moses put it more graphically when he said, "The foreigner who comes from a distant land, when they see the plagues of the land and the diseases with which the Lord has afflicted it, will say, 'All its land is brimstone and salt, a burning waste, unsown and unproductive, and no grass grows in it'" (Deut. 29:22–23). We will talk more about this later when we look at the prophecies of the present.

The fourth prophecy is God also says, "Yes, I will disperse you, but I will preserve you." The preservation of the Jews is one of the greatest miracles of God in history. What do we read in the Old Testament? Every nation came against Israel. The Ammonites, the Hittites, the Philistines, the Chaldeans, and etc., attacked them. But where are these nations today? Where are the Chaldeans and Philistines? They are in the dust bed of history. Where are the Jews? Regathered in the land of Palestine. God dispersed them for two thousand years; they have been wondering all over the face of the earth. And yet for two thousand years, they have been able to keep their identity. There is no other nation in all the history of mankind that has been dispersed like that and has been able to keep their identity. Every year the Jews would say, "Next year in Jerusalem!" as they celebrated the Passover. God kept that alive in their hearts, and God promised that He would do it. Let me show you an example.

In Jeremiah 31:35–37, here is God's promise about the preservation of the Jewish people. "Thus, says the Lord." Here is God's signature. I love this. Whenever God gets ready to say something that is important, and this happens a lot in scripture, He gives His signature. Verse 35 is the signature of God. "Thus says the Lord, Who Gives the sun for light by day, and the fixed order of the moon and the stars for light by night, Who stirs up the sea so that its waves roar; the Lord of Host is His name: [Does everybody know which God we are talking about?] If this fixed order departs from before Me, declares the Lord, Then the offspring of Israel shall cease from being a nation before Me forever." (Then He emphasizes it.) "Thus says the Lord, 'If the heavens above can be measured, and the foundation of the earth searched out below, Then I will cast off all the offspring of Israel for all that they have done.' Declares the Lord." When will Israel cease to be a nation? When the sun stops coming up, and the seasons stop. That is when the Jewish people will cease from being a nation. Scientists are telling us that they are finding new galaxies all the time. That is very strong language.

"But Zion said, 'The Lord has forsaken me, and the Lord has forgotten me'" (Isa. 49:14–16). That is what the Jewish people have been saying. But look what God says in verse 15: "Can a woman forget her nursing child, and have no compassion on the son of her womb?" (God is asking the question, "Can a woman forget her nursing child?" But He recognizes that they possibly can forget.) "Even these may forget, but I will not forget you. Behold, I have inscribed you [literally means tattooed you] on the palm of my hands." God said, "I will disperse you, and I will preserve you," and God did both, and God has been faithful to His Word and to Israel.

Prophecies Being Fulfilled Now

God says a time is coming when I will regather the children of Israel from the four corners of the earth. I am going to disperse you, I will preserve you, and then I am going to regather you from the four corners of the earth. This is mentioned more than any other prophecy. Here is just one of those prophesies: Isaiah 11:10–12. He is talking about the end times. "Then it will come about in that day that the nations will resort to the root of Jesse." (That is the house of David. He is talking about the Messiah.) "Who will stand as a signal [banner, flag] for the people; and His resting place will be glorious. Then it will happen on that day that the Lord will again recover the second time with His hand. [A second time the first time was the regathering from Babylonian captivity. This is the second time.] Will again recover the second time with His hand the remnant of His people, who will remain, from Assyria, Egypt, Pathros, Cush, Elam, Shinar, Hamath, and from the Islands of the sea. [Which is a Jewish phrase for the whole world.] And He will lift up a standard [flag, banner] for the nations, and will assemble the banished ones from Israel [that is the ten tribes from the northern kingdom] and will gather the dispersed of Judah [that is the two tribes from the southern kingdom] from the four corners of the earth."

The return from Babylon was forty thousand Jews who were mainly from Judah. This is talking about the regathering of Israel and Judah from the four corners of the earth, a second regathering. This is going to be a regathering in unbelief. The Jews in Israel today are not there in belief. Eighty percent of them don't believe in God, or they are agnostic, 17 percent believe in God, and only 3 percent are orthodox.

I have mentioned being in Israel in December. While we were at the Knesset, we were given a tour. Our tour guide was explaining a beautiful mural that had three panels of Israel's past, present, and future represented. In the future panel, it had a depiction of Isaiah 11:6–9:

> And the wolf will dwell with the lamb, And the leopard will lie down with the young goat, And the calf and the young lion and the fatling together; And

a little boy will lead them. Also the cow and the bear will graze, Their young will lie down together, And the lion will eat straw like the ox. The nursing child will play by the hole of the cobra, And the weaned child will put his hand on the viper's den. They will not hurt or destroy in all My holy mountain, For the earth will be full of the knowledge of the LORD As the waters cover the sea.[5]

The mural showed what is described in Isaiah 11. She said, "We really don't know what the artist is trying to say, but we will leave that up to your interpretation." I leaned over to one of the others who was on the Israel trip with me, and said, "She is a secular Jew." And that is exactly who she was, one of the 80 percent who are secular Jews and are there for nationalism.

Verse 12 says that they will lift up a flag, and it also tells what will be on the flag. Have you ever seen a Jewish flag? It has a blue bow at the top and a blue bow at the bottom and in the center is the Mogen David. We think of Mogen David as a wine. But it is the Star of David. Look what it says will be on it in: "The root of the house of David." The Star of David will be on the flag. It has been like a magnet drawing the Jews back home.

God said, "I will also reestablish your nation of Israel." This is probably one of the greatest miracles of this century. Most of us have never known a world without Israel. People laughed and scoffed at the idea that Israel would ever exist again. Finally, on May 14, 1948, a group of Zionist got on the radio in Tel Aviv, and they announced to the world the birth of the Jewish state. The world died laughing. Do you know why? There were only five hundred thousand Jews in all the land—men, women, and children. They had one airplane and an old biplane, and they did not have any bombs. They dropped Molotov cocktails out the cockpit. The only guns they had were from the Warsaw ghetto, and they were handguns.

The next morning, May 15, 1948, they were attacked by six nations simultaneously, representing one hundred million Arabs. The odds were two hundred to one. The Lebanese came from the North, the Syrians from the Northeast, Iraq came from the East, the Jordanians came across the Jordan River in the greatest assault of all led by British army officers, the best army in the Middle East. Saudi Arabia came from the Southeast, and the Egyptian army came in two columns. The largest army headed toward Jerusalem, the other headed toward Tel Aviv. And before they left Egypt, the king of Egypt announced that within one week, they will have pushed the Jews into the Mediterranean Sea, and the Arabs will be dancing in the streets of Tel Aviv.

The world laughed, but when you have the Lord of host fighting for you, you don't have to have any guns or bombs. God proved that with David and Goliath. This is David and Goliath all over again. Within three months, the Arab nations came with their hat in their hands, begging for a cease-fire. And by that time, the Israelis had conquered almost all of the entire land of Palestine. This was a great miracle of modern man. Unless you understand the circumstances, you will not understand one of the great prophecies of God.

Isaiah 66:7 is about the birth of Israel, or I should say the rebirth of Israel. "Before she travailed, she brought forth"; that is kind of unusual, isn't it? Do you know what it is saying? It is saying that before the woman went into labor, she delivered. Look what else it says: "Before her pain came, she gave birth to a boy" (Isa. 66:7). (Well, who has heard of such a thing? Well, look at the next thing the prophet proclaims.) "Who has heard of such a thing? Who has seen such a thing? Can a land be born in one day? Can a nation be brought forth all at once?" The answer is yes; it happened May 14, 1948. Do you know what happened? The day after the nation was born, the birth pains began. It was the next day that the Arab nations attacked with The War of 1948.

Do you know what was one of the keys to the survival of Israel in 1948? Eleven minutes after the state of Israel was proclaimed, President Harry Truman was at a microphone recognizing the existence of the State of Israel, and money and arms began to flow to Israel from the United States. What is so amazing about that decision is that state department papers now reveal that there was not one person in the whole USA's government that favored the recognition of Israel. Everyone told Harry Truman not to recognize Israel because we would make the Arabs mad. Do you know what happened?

Before Harry Truman was president, he owned a haberdashery that went bankrupt. Harry's business partner was a Jew—Eddie Jacobson. The night before Israel was to declare their independence, Harry Truman's old business partner from Independence, Missouri, came to see him. He said, "Harry, I have never asked anything of you since you have been president of the United States, even though I am one of your best friends. But I am going to ask something of you now. I believe that when you were in your mother's womb, God called you to play a major role in world history by recognizing the existence of the State of Israel. And tomorrow, I would like for you to do that for the Jewish people." How do you say no to that? And against all the advice of all of his advisers, Harry Truman was at the microphone eleven minutes after the declaration and declared the existence of the State of Israel.

Isn't that amazing? Of course, Harry Truman had other motivations as well. In 1948, Harry Truman was up for reelection. He was not supposed to win. Remember they published the headlines before the election was finished: Dewey Defeats Truman! Harry Truman wasn't dropped off a turnip truck. He knew there were more Jews in New York City than in the whole nation of Israel. But whatever His motivation was, God's timing was perfect. He stepped in, and he recognized Israel, and the arms and money flowed, and the State of Israel prevailed. We have the regathering of the Jewish people, we have the reestablishment of the nation of Israel, and the third prophecy is the reclamation of the land.

The reclamation of the land is another miracle of God. Isaiah 35:1–7 and Joel 2:21–26 shows the reclamation of the land in great detail.

> The wilderness and the desert will be glad, And the Arabah will rejoice and blossom; Like the crocus It will blossom profusely And rejoice with rejoicing and shout of joy. The glory of Lebanon will be given to it, The majesty of Carmel and Sharon. They will see the glory of the LORD, The majesty of our God. Encourage the exhausted, and strengthen the feeble. Say to those with anxious heart, "Take courage, fear not. Behold, your God will come *with* vengeance; The recompense of God will come, But He will save you." Then the eyes of the blind will be opened And the ears of the deaf will be unstopped. Then the lame will leap like a deer, And the tongue of the mute will shout for joy. For waters will break forth in the wilderness And streams in the Arabah. The scorched land will become a pool And the thirsty ground springs of water; In the haunt of jackals, its resting place, Grass *becomes* reeds and rushes.[6] (Isa. 35:1–7)

Do not fear, O land, rejoice and be glad, For the LORD has done great things. Do not fear, beasts of the field, For the pastures of the wilderness have turned green, For the tree has borne its fruit, The fig tree and the vine have yielded in full. So rejoice, O sons of Zion, And be glad in the LORD your God; For He has given you the *L*early rain for *your* vindication. And He has poured down for you the rain, The early and *L*latter rain as before. The threshing floors will be full of grain, And the vats will overflow with the new wine and oil. "Then I will make up to you for the years That the swarming locust has eaten, The creeping locust, the stripping locust and the gnawing locust, My great army which I sent among you. You will have plenty to eat and be satisfied And praise the name of the LORD your God, Who has dealt wondrously with you; Then My people will never be put to shame."[7] (Joel 2:21–26)

These verses talk about when God brings the Jews back the land will blossom, and the desert will bloom. It talks about how the land will be reclaimed. Unless you have studied the history of Israel, you cannot begin to appreciate what has happened there, and you cannot begin to appreciate the miracles of God.

The land of Israel, for two thousand years, has been under foreign conquerors. Then finally, the Jews got hold of the land, and God began to bless the land. At the end of 1900, that land was raped. Do you know how many trees were in Israel in 1900? Seventeen thousand. Do you know how we know that? The land of Israel was under the Turks, and Turks taxed trees. If you had too big of a tax bill, you went out and cut down a tree. There were only seventeen thousand trees in the whole land of Israel.

When we read the Old Testament, we read of great forest full of all kinds of wildlife. Do you know that in 1900, most of the land was a barren desert? Go back and look in old Bibles, and what do you see? You see some pictures of the Holy Land, and you always see some guy standing in the middle of the desert. It was the most godforsaken place on the earth. It couldn't even support the few people that were living there. Then the Jew began to come back in 1900, and from 1900 to 1948, the Jews began to work to reclaim the land.

The first thing that they did was to go into the valleys: The valley of Aijalon (where the sun stood still for Joshua), the valley of Sharon, the valley of Jezreel (or Armageddon), and the valley of Gulock. Those valleys were malaria-infested swamplands; nobody would even go near them. The Jews went to Australia and brought back thousands of eucalyptus trees, and they planted those trees all around the perimeter of those swamps because the eucalyptus tree soaks up more water than any tree known to man. The roots acted like a sponge, and they soaked up the water. Then they went in with modern engineering, and they drained those swamplands. And today, those four valleys are the most agricultural productive pieces of landscape on the face of God's earth.

Since 1948, Israel has become one of a few nations in the world that exports food. Almost any day, you will see trucks lined up taking agricultural products into Jordan. Israel is feeding that part of the world. And it is all because God has poured out His grace and mercy upon them. In the valley of Sharon, on one side are peanut fields and cotton fields, on the other side a banana plantation. How do you grow bananas in the same place you grow cotton and peanuts? I don't know. They have strawberry fields and avocados and everything imaginable growing year round. They have tapped the Sea of Galilee, and they have pumped out the water in a concrete channel that runs the entire length of the nation of Israel. It goes down into the Negev Desert, and now the desert is blooming. They are farming the desert just as Isaiah 35 says. The whole land has come alive.

In the Jerusalem Peace Forest, they have replanted trees. Do you know how many trees they have planted since 1900? More than three hundred million trees. Do you know what that has done to the climate? It has increased the rainfall by 450 percent. The land is flowing with milk and honey again. While in Israel in December of 2013, our guide told us that countries are wanting to buy Israeli cows and bees because the bees produce more honey than other bees, and the cows produce more milk than other cows. God said, "I am going to reclaim the land," and God has been faithful to His word.

The fourth thing is God said that He would revive the language. "For then I will give to the people purified lips, that all of them may call upon the name of the Lord, to serve Him shoulder to shoulder" (Zeph. 3:9). The rabbis have always said that this passage of Scripture means that God is going to restore the Hebrew language for the Jewish people. They always thought that would occur when the Lord came to reign during the millennium kingdom, but Israel got a jump on it.

In the mid 1800s, there was a man by the name of Eliezer Ben-Yehuda (1858–1922). There is a street named for him in almost every city in Israel, Ben Yehuda Street. That is how important this man is to Israel. God put a vision in this man's mind and heart. It was a vision to revive the Hebrew language. The Hebrew language had not been spoken for nearly two thousand years. When the Jews were dispersed, the Jews that went to Europe took the Hebrew language and mixed it with German and came up with Yiddish. The Jews that went to the Mediterranean Basin, they took the Hebrew language and mixed it with Spanish and came up with Ladino. They spoke mongrelized languages. The only place in the world where Hebrew was spoken was in the synagogues when the Scriptures were read.

God gave this man a vision of reviving the Hebrew language. He was one of the most determined men I ever read about. He came down with tuberculosis at the age of twenty and was given about a month to live. He said, "If I am going to die, I am going to die in Israel." He went to Israel in the 1800s, which was one of the worst places on the face of the earth a sick person should go. Malaria, tuberculosis, everything was rampant there. He went there, and he died when he was sixty-four years old. He went through two wives; he worked both of them to death because he never worked to earn a living. His wives worked to earn a living because he said that he had been called of God to revive the Hebrew language.

He would work day and night, sometimes eighteen hours a day, trying to revive the Hebrew language. Have you ever stopped to think about what it would be like to try to revive a language that had been dead for nearly two thousand years? He had to come up with a word for everything that happened during that time and every invention. He was a purist; he would not take the word *telegraph* and move it over into the Hebrew language. It had to be a Hebrew word, so he would take root words and study the roots and put them together and come up with a pure Hebrew word for *telegraph*. He put together nineteen huge volumes on the Hebrew language before he died.

Everybody opposed him! The Zionists were opposed to him because the Zionists were all atheist and agnostics. And they said that they did not want to speak a religious language. And the orthodox were opposed to him because they said this is a religious language and not a language for the streets. Everybody opposed him. He said that he was going to revive the language anyway.

This man was such a fanatic that his wife, after being married for several years, said, "Everybody is talking about us because we don't have a child." Now in a Jewish family, that is a big deal. She said, "Can we have a child?"

He said, "We can have a child when you learn biblical Hebrew."

She said, "What do you mean?"

He said, "We are going to have the first true Jew born in two thousand years. When my son is born, nobody is going to speak to him for seven years except in biblical Hebrew."

So she went to work and learned biblical Hebrew; it took her three years. She then conceived a child, and for seven years, no one was allowed in his presence that could not speak biblical Hebrew. There were only about five people who could at that time. His son was turned lose on the streets, and he could not talk to anybody. He later had daughters, and he would not allow them to marry unless the future husband learned biblical Hebrew. Then they had to pass the test he gave them before they could marry his daughters. This man was serious.

Do you know what happened on May 14, 1948? There were five hundred thousand Jews coming from more than 140 different countries, speaking more than 120 different languages, and none of them wanted biblical Hebrew.

They all hated biblical Hebrew, but they said that there was no other way that they could communicate. It means that the Jews can open their Bibles, and they can read the Scriptures in the original language. God did that because He is preparing their hearts to accept Jesus Christ as their Messiah. They will be able to see in the prophecies of Jesus and see their fulfillment in their original language.

The fifth prophecy is the reoccupation of the city of Jerusalem. I consider this to be one of the most important of all the prophecies. The Word says that the Jew will be in Jerusalem when the Lord comes back. That occurred on June of 1967 when the Jews reoccupied the city of Jerusalem. In Luke 21:24–25, this is the same speech that Luke records for the church as Matthew (24) did for the Jews. And Luke gives us some information that Matthew's Gospel does not supply. "And they will fall by the edge of the sword and will be led captive and to all the nations." Did that happen? Yes! Forty years after Jesus's resurrection, Titus, the Roman leader in 70 AD, came in, and they massacred the Jews, they tore down the temple, and they took all the survivors into captivity all over the world. That was exactly what Jesus prophesied. "And they will fall by the edge of the sword, and will be led captive into all the nations; and Jerusalem will be trampled underfoot by the Gentiles until the times of the Gentiles be fulfilled" (Luke 21:24–25). Did Jesus mean what He said? I think He meant exactly what He said. Jerusalem will be trampled underfoot until the times of the Gentiles are fulfilled. When the Romans got through, the Byzantines took over. When the Byzantines took over, the Mamluks came in. When the Mamluks got through, the Arabs took over. The Arabs were followed by the Crusaders. The Crusaders were followed by the Arabs again. The Arabs were followed by the Turks. The Turks were followed by the British. The British were followed by the Jordanians. Until June of 1967, in that miraculous Six-Day War, the Jews retook the city of Jerusalem for the first time in 1,897 years!

The Word of God says Jerusalem shall be trampled underfoot until the times of the Gentiles are complete. The times of the Gentiles has been fulfilled! We are living on borrowed time. The Jews are back in the land, and the Jews have the city of Jerusalem. On the very day that the Jewish commandos conquered the ancient city of Jerusalem, those commandos went to the Wailing Wall and fell on their knees, and they were weeping and crying. Rabbi Shouam Goram, the chief rabbi of the Israeli army, came up to the wall with his army and took out a ram's horn, which is a sign of the Messiah, and blew that horn. He raised his hands, and everyone quieted down. The first words he spoke (this is a rabbi, an orthodox rabbi), "I proclaimed to you the beginning of the Messianic Age." Why did he say that? Because he has read the prophets. All the prophets say that the Messiah is going to come back when the Jews are back in the land and the Jews are back in the city of Jerusalem.

He thinks it is going to be the first time; boy, is he in for a surprise. But at least he has the spiritual sensitivity to know that the Messiah is coming soon!

Have you ever stopped to think about the fact that the first time Jesus came, it was the Jews who were spiritually blind, and it was the Gentiles that recognized Him as the Messiah? Jesus is getting ready to come back again, and it is the Orthodox Jews that are saying the Messiah is coming! The Messiah is coming! And the church is sitting around and saying, "What else is new?" We are the ones that are spiritually blind today. We do not know the Old Testament well enough to know what the Hebrew prophets have said. Jesus is coming back soon! *Maranatha*! Our Lord comes!

The sixth prophecy is the resurgence of the Israeli military. God says that He is going to bring Israel back home, but also, He is going to resurge their military. Think what a miracle this is. Do you know that Israel is the fourth world power behind the United States of America, the Soviet Union, and China? This country is only one hundred miles from the top of the Sea of Galilee to the bottom of the Dead Sea. You can drive all over Israel in one day's time. This country is the size of New Jersey. It is one of the smallest countries on the face of the earth. It is a postage-stamp-sized country, and yet it is the fourth military power.

> In that day I will make the clans of Judah like a firepot among pieces of wood and a flaming torch among sheaves, so they will consume on the right

> hand and on the left all the surrounding people, while
> the inhabitants of Jerusalem again dwell on their own
> sites in Jerusalem.[8] (Zech. 12:6)

Notice the Jews are back in Jerusalem, and they will be like a blazing firepot devouring to the right and to the left. That is the resurgence of the Israeli military.

In 1982, we saw the power of the Israeli military. For seven years, the PLO were shooting rockets into the Golan Heights, using seven SAM (surface-to-air missiles) missile sites located in Syria, killing innocent men, women, and children. The Israelis begged the United Nations to do something about it for seven years, but they refused and basically said it is not their problem. The Israelites decided that they would do something about it. As the military leaders met, they decided that it would take one hundred planes, and they would probably lose twenty-five planes and pilots, but they would take out all seven of the SAM missile sites. They debated losing twenty-five of their best pilots and planes, and they decided it was worth it to stop the senseless killing of their citizens.

The one hundred planes took off early in the morning to carry out their mission. They were not in the air for very long when they radioed back that they were being met by one hundred Russian-made Syrian MIGS. Now they would lose fifty planes, and they might not get to all seven of the SAM missile sites. The team leader asked if they should turn around or continue with their plan. The word was given to proceed. They fought all day long, because the battle only lasted one day. At the end of the day, seven SAM missile sites were destroyed, eighty-two Russian-made Syrian MIGS knocked out of the sky—destroyed, not one Israeli plane was destroyed.

People say, "Aren't those Israelis good pilots?" Yes, they are, but when you have the Lord of host fighting for you, you can prevail against astronomical odds. Military leaders consider this one of the greatest miracles and battle plan to be studied in the future. God said He would allow the Israeli army to reemerge on the world scene as a powerful force, and that is what He has done.

Next is the refocusing of world politics upon the nation of Israel. "And it will come about in that day that I will make Jerusalem a heavy stone for all the people; all who lift it will be severely injured [That literally means herniated]. And all the nations of the earth will be gathered against it" (Zech. 12:3). This prophecy says that all the nations of the world will come against Israel. Israel is one of the smallest countries on the face of the earth, and it is the focal point of world politics. It happened overnight in 1973. Do you know how? The Arabs pulled an oil boycott, and the Western nations were brought to their knees, and they went to the Arabs and said, "We need oil."

The Arabs said, "We will give it to you, but you will have to pay two prices: (1) you are going to pay four times more for it than you have ever paid before; and (2) you must line up with us in our obsession to annihilate the nation of Israel. And overnight, the United Nations voted against Israel. And overnight, the Western world turned against Israel. And overnight, Israel became the focal point of world politics. Why? Because Satan hates Israel; they are God's chosen people. And God says that a time is coming when He will bring a remnant of them to salvation in Jesus Christ. Just as Satan tried to destroy Jesus at His birth by sending Herod's army to destroy the babies of Bethlehem, Satan is trying to destroy the Jewish people so that prophecies cannot be fulfilled. He does not want one Jew in Israel to be saved. He tried to do it with Hitler, he is trying to do it with the Arabs, and he will continue to try to eliminate Israel. Satan hates the Jews; that is why throughout history, he has tried to wipe them out.

The Prophecies Concerning the Future

I have really already spoken of these. Let me just very quickly go over them. *Tribulation.* God says that I am regathering the Jewish people for a purpose: to put them in the tribulation. "When you are in distress and all these things have come upon you, in the latter days you will return to the LORD your God and listen to His voice" (Deut. 4:30). The Bible teaches that there are seven years of tribulation coming upon the earth. Those seven years, although it will affect all the earth, are primarily focused at the Jewish people. It is the last week of Daniel's prophecy that God is going to work through the Jewish people. That seven-year period is recorded in great detail in the book of Revelation chapters 4–19. The Jews have rejected Jesus as their Messiah, and God is going to pound their hardened hearts with His wrath until, finally, some of their hearts are broken, and they come to a saving knowledge of Jesus Christ as their Messiah. Zechariah 13:8 says that two-thirds of all the Jews will die during the tribulation. "And it will come about in all the Land, Declares the Lord, 'That two parts in it will be cut off and perish; but the third will be left in it.'" It will make the Nazi Holocaust look like a Sunday school picnic. One-third of the Jews will live to the end of the tribulation period. God says that He is going to put you in tribulation, and two-thirds of you will be destroyed because they refuse to acknowledge Jesus as the Christ. God says a remnant of one-third of the Jews will live to the end.

Salvation is the second prophecy in the future to be fulfilled.

> And I will pour out on the house of David and on the inhabitants of Jerusalem, the Spirit of grace and supplication, so that they will look on Me whom they have pierced. They will mourn for Him, as one mourns for an only son, and they will weep bitterly over Him, like the bitter weeping over a first-born. (Zech. 12:10)
>
> A remnant will be saved.[9] (Rom. 9:27)

What is He saying? That remnant will look upon Him whom they have pierced, and they will weep and wail and mourn as you would weep over the loss of an only child. They are going to be brought to repentance, and they will be brought to salvation. Look at Zechariah 13:1: "In that day a fountain will be opened for the house of David and for the inhabitants of Jerusalem, for sin and for impurity."

Tribulation, Salvation, and Primacy or Regathering. Only this time, it will be a regathering in belief. The first thing that Jesus is going to do when He comes back to this earth is that He is going to regather every Jew on the face of this earth who has accepted Him as Lord and Savior to the nation of Israel. Deuteronomy 30:1–9 and Ezekiel 36:22–30 speaks of this.

> So it shall be when all of these things have come upon you, the blessing and the curse which I have set before you, and you call *them* to mind in all nations where the LORD your God has banished you, and you return to the LORD your God and obey Him with all your heart and soul according to all that I command you today, you and your sons, then the LORD your God will restore you from captivity, and have compassion on you, and will gather you again from all the peoples where the LORD your God has scattered you. If your outcasts are at the ends of the earth, from there the LORD your God will gather you, and from there He will bring you back.[5] The LORD your God will bring you into the land which your fathers possessed, and

you shall possess it; and He will prosper you and multiply you more than your fathers. Moreover the LORD your God will circumcise your heart and the heart of your descendants, to love the LORD your God with all your heart and with all your soul, so that you may live. The LORD your God will inflict all these curses on your enemies and on those who hate you, who persecuted you. And you shall again obey the LORD, and observe all His commandments which I command you today. Then the LORD your God will prosper you abundantly in all the work of your hand, in the offspring of your body and in the offspring of your cattle and in the produce of your ground, for the LORD will again rejoice over you for good, just as He rejoiced over your fathers.[10] (Deut. 30:1–9)

Therefore say to the house of Israel, "Thus says the Lord GOD, 'It is not for your sake, O house of Israel, that I am about to act, but for My holy name, which you have profaned among the nations where you went. I will vindicate the holiness of My great name which has been profaned among the nations, which you have profaned in their midst. Then the nations will know that I am the LORD,' declares the Lord GOD, 'when I prove Myself holy among you in their sight. For I will take you from the nations, gather you from all the lands and bring you into your own land. Then I will sprinkle clean water on you, and you will be clean; I will cleanse you from all your filthiness and from all your idols. Moreover, I will give you a new heart and

> put a new spirit within you; and I will remove the
> heart of stone from your flesh and give you a heart of
> flesh. I will put My Spirit within you and cause you to
> walk in My statutes, and you will be careful to observe
> My ordinances. You will live in the land that I gave to
> your forefathers; so you will be My people, and I will
> be your God. Moreover, I will save you from all your
> uncleanness; and I will call for the grain and multiply
> it, and I will not bring a famine on you. I will multiply
> the fruit of the tree and the produce of the field, so
> that you will not receive again the disgrace of famine
> among the nations. Then you will remember your evil
> ways and your deeds that were not good, and you will
> loathe yourselves in your own sight for your iniquities
> and your abominations. I am not doing *this* for your
> sake,' declares the Lord GOD, 'let it be known to you.
> Be ashamed and confounded for your ways, O house
> of Israel!'"[11] (Ezek. 36:22–30)

The regathering that is going on now is a regathering in unbelief, and then there will be a gathering in belief. Then God will fulfill the promises He has made to the Jewish people, all of those which have never been fulfilled because they have been in rebellion to God.

To the remnant that has accepted Jesus, He will make them the prime nation of the world. There the Lord will reign. The Old Testament says that at that time, the kings of the earth will bring their wealth and their riches to Jerusalem. And foreigners will come and rebuild your cities, and the Gentiles of the world will serve you. God is going to turn this world upside down. Because right now, the Jews are the objects of hatred, contempt, and prejudice. Look what is going to happen when the Jew is made the prime nation of the world. "So many people and mighty nations will come to seek the Lord of Host in Jerusalem and to entreat the favor of the Lord. Thus says the Lord of Host, 'In those days ten men from all the nations will grasp the garment of a Jew saying, "Let us go with you, for we have heard that God is with you"'" (Zech. 8:22–23). The Gentiles will say, "Let us just walk along the road next to you because we know that God is with you."

Sometimes, when I speak on the promises to the Jewish people, people say, "Oh, you make me want to be a Jew." I say, "No, you don't want to be a Jew, because if you were a Jew, the odds are that you would have that veil over your eyes as well. And you might never come to salvation in Jesus Christ." God has made some beautiful and mighty promises to the Jews. But He has made some promises to the church that are beautiful as well, and we don't need to covet promises that are made to the Jews.

The Word of God says that those who are Christians when they die, that our spirit never lose consciousness ("But I am hard-pressed from both *directions,* having the desire to depart and be with Christ, for *that* is very much better" [Phil. 1:23].). Instead, our conscious spirits are immediately ushered into the presence of Jesus by his holy angels ("We are of good courage, I say, and prefer rather to be absent from the body and to be at home with the Lord" [2 Cor. 5:8].). Our spirits remain in the Lord's presence until He appears for his church. At that time, He brings our spirits with Him, resurrects our bodies, reunites our spirit with our bodies, and then glorifies our bodies, perfecting them and rendering them eternal.

> But we do not want you to be uninformed, brethren, about those who are asleep, so that you will not grieve as do the rest who have no hope. For if we believe that Jesus died and rose again, even so God will bring with Him those who have fallen asleep in Jesus. For this we say to you by the word of the Lord, that we who are alive and remain until the coming of the Lord, will not precede those who have fallen asleep. For the Lord Himself will descend from heaven with a shout, with the voice of *the* archangel and with the trumpet of God, and the dead in Christ will rise first. Then we who are alive and remain will be caught up together with them in the clouds to meet the Lord in the air, and so we shall always be with the Lord. Therefore comfort one another with these words.[12] (1 Thess. 4:13–18)

We return with Him to heaven in our glorified bodies where we are judged for our works to determine our degree of rewards—not salvation ("I *did* not at all *mean* with the immoral people of this world, or with the covetous and swindlers, or with idolaters, for then you would have to go out of the world" [2 Cor. 5:10].). When this judgment is completed, we participate in a glorious wedding feast to celebrate the union of Jesus and His bride, the church ("Let us rejoice and be glad and give the glory to Him, for the marriage of the Lamb has come and His bride has made herself ready." It was given to her to clothe herself in fine linen, bright *and* clean; for the fine linen is the righteous acts of the saints. Then he said* to me, 'Write, "Blessed are those who are invited to the marriage supper of the Lamb."' And he said* to me, 'These are true words of God'" [Rev. 19:7–9].). At the conclusion of the feast, we burst from the heavens with Jesus, returning with Him to the earth in glory ("And the armies which are in heaven, clothed in fine linen, white *and* clean, were following Him on white horses" [Rev. 19:14].). We witness His victory at Armageddon, we shout hallelujah! As He is crowned the King of kings and the Lord of lords, and we revel in His glory as He begins to reign over all the earth from Mount Zion in Jerusalem.

> Behold, a day is coming for the LORD when the spoil taken from you will be divided among you. For I will gather all the nations against Jerusalem to battle, and the city will be captured, the houses plundered, the women ravished and half of the city exiled, but the rest of the people will not be cut off from the city. Then the LORD will go forth and fight against those nations, as when He fights on a day of battle. In that

day His feet will stand on the Mount of Olives, which is in front of Jerusalem on the east; and the Mount of Olives will be split in its middle from east to west by a very large valley, so that half of the mountain will move toward the north and the other half toward the south. You will flee by the valley of My mountains, for the valley of the mountains will reach to Azel; yes, you will flee just as you fled before the earthquake in the days of Uzziah king of Judah. Then the LORD, my God, will come, *and* all the holy ones with Him! In that day there will be no light; the luminaries will dwindle. For it will be a unique day which is known to the LORD, neither day nor night, but it will come about that at evening time there will be light. And in that day living waters will flow out of Jerusalem, half of them toward the eastern sea and the other half toward the western sea; it will be in summer as well as in winter. And the LORD will be king over all the earth; in that day the LORD will be *the only* one, and His name *the only* one.[13] (Zech. 14:1–9)

Then I saw an angel standing in the sun, and he cried out with a loud voice, saying to all the birds which fly in midheaven, "Come, assemble for the great supper of God, so that you may eat the flesh of kings and the flesh of ᶠcommanders and the flesh of mighty men and the flesh of horses and of those who sit on them and the flesh of all men, both free men and slaves, and small and great." And I saw the beast and the kings of the earth and their armies assembled to make war against Him who sat on the horse and against His army. And the beast was seized, and with him the false prophet who performed the signs in his presence, by which he deceived those who had received the mark of the beast and those who worshiped his image; these two were thrown alive into the lake of fire which burns with brimstone. And the rest were killed with the sword which came from the mouth of Him who sat on the horse, and all the birds were filled with their flesh.[14] (Rev. 19:17–21)

For one thousand years, we participate in that reign, assisting Jesus with the instruction, administration, and enforcement of His perfect laws.

Then I saw an angel coming down from heaven, holding the key of the abyss and a great chain in his hand. And he laid hold of the dragon, the serpent of old, who is the devil and Satan, and bound him for a thousand years; and he threw him into the abyss, and shut *it* and sealed *it* over him, so that he would not deceive the nations any longer, until the thousand years were completed; after these things he must be released for a short time. Then I saw thrones, and they sat on them, and judgment was given to them. And I *saw* the souls of those who had been beheaded because of their testimony of Jesus and because of the word of God, and those who had not worshiped the beast or his image, and had not received the mark on their forehead and on their hand; and they came to life and reigned with Christ for a thousand years. The rest of the dead did not come to life until the thousand years were completed. This is the first resurrection. Blessed and holy is the one who has a part in the first resurrection; over these the second death has no power, but they will be priests of God and of Christ and will reign with Him for a thousand years.[15] (Rev. 20:1–6)

We will see the earth regenerated and nature reconciled.

And the wolf will dwell with the lamb, And the leopard will lie down with the young goat, And the calf and the young lion and the fatling together; And a little boy will lead them. Also the cow and the bear will graze, Their young will lie down together, And the lion will eat straw like the ox. The nursing child will play by the hole of the cobra, And the weaned child will put his hand on the viper's den. They will not hurt or destroy in all My holy mountain, For the earth will be full of the knowledge of the LORD As the waters cover the sea.[16] (Isa. 11:6–9)

We will see holiness abound and the earth flooded with peace, righteousness, and justice.

And it will come about in the last days That the mountain of the house of the LORD Will be established as the chief of the mountains. It will be raised above the hills, And the peoples will stream to it. Many nations will come and say, "Come and let us go up to the mountain of the LORD And to the house of the God of Jacob, That He may teach us about His ways And that we may walk in His paths." For from Zion will go forth the law, Even the word of the LORD from Jerusalem. And He will judge between many peoples And render decisions for mighty, distant nations. Then they will hammer their swords into plowshares And their spears into pruning hooks; Nation will not lift up sword against nation, And never again will they train for war. Each of them will sit under his vine And under his fig tree, With no one to make *them* afraid, For the mouth of the LORD of hosts has spoken. Though all the peoples walk Each in the name of his god, As for us, we will walk In the name of the LORD our God forever and ever. "In that day," declares the LORD, "I will assemble the lame And gather the outcasts, Even those whom I have afflicted. I will make the lame a remnant And the outcasts a strong nation," And the LORD will reign over them in Mount Zion From now on and forever.[17] (Mic. 4:1–7)

At the end of the millennium, we will witness the release of Satan to deceive the nations. We see the truly despicable nature of the heart of man as millions rally to Satan in his attempt to overthrow the throne of Jesus. But we will shout "Hallelujah!" again when we witness God's supernatural destruction of Satan's armies and see Satan himself cast into hell, where he will be tormented forever.

> When the thousand years are completed, Satan will be released from his prison, and will come out to deceive the nations which are in the four corners of the earth, Gog and Magog, to gather them together for the war; the number of them is like the sand of the seashore. And they came up on the broad plain of the earth and surrounded the camp of the saints and the beloved city, and fire came down from heaven and devoured them. And the devil who deceived them was thrown into the lake of fire and brimstone, where the beast and the false prophet are also; and they will be tormented day and night forever and ever.[18] (Rev. 20:7–10)

We will next witness the great white throne judgment when the unrighteous are resurrected to stand before God. We will see perfect holiness and justice in action as God pronounces His terrible judgment upon this congregation of the damned, who have rejected His gift of love and mercy in Jesus Christ ("Then I saw a great white throne and Him who sat upon it, from whose presence earth and heaven fled away, and no place was found for them. And I saw the dead, the great and the small, standing before the throne, and books were opened; and another book was opened, which is *the book* of life; and the dead were judged from the things which were written in the books, according to their deeds. And the sea gave up the dead which were in it, and death and Hades gave up the dead which were in them; and they were judged, every one *of them* according to their deeds" [Rev. 20:11–13].). Jesus will be fully vindicated as every knee shall bow and every tongue confesses that he is Lord. Then the unrighteous will receive their just reward as they are cast into hell ("Then death and Hades were thrown into the lake of fire. This is the second death, the lake of fire. And if anyone's name was not found written in the book of life, he was thrown into the lake of fire" [Rev. 20:14–15].).

We will then witness the most spectacular fireworks display in all of history. We will be taken to the New Jerusalem, the eternal mansion prepared by Jesus for His bride, and from there, we will watch as God renovates this earth with fire, burning away all the filth and pollution left by Satan's last battle ("Looking for and hastening the coming of the day of God, because of which the heavens will be destroyed by burning, and the elements will melt with intense heat! But according to His promise we are looking for new heavens and a new earth, in which righteousness dwells" [2 Pet. 3:12–13].). Just as the angels rejoiced when God created the universe, we will rejoice as we watch God superheat this earth and reshape it like a hot ball of wax into the new earth, the eternal earth, the paradise where we will live forever in the presence of God ("Then I saw a new heaven and a new earth; for the first heaven and the first earth passed away, and there is no longer *any* sea" [Rev. 21:1].).

What a glorious moment it will be when we are lowered to the new earth inside the fabulous New Jerusalem ("And I saw the holy city, new Jerusalem, coming down out of heaven from God, made ready as a bride adorned for her husband" [Rev. 21:2].). (God will come down from heaven to dwell with us.) ("And I heard a loud voice from the throne, saying, 'Behold, the tabernacle of God is among men, and He will dwell among them, and they shall be His people, and God Himself will be among them'" [Rev. 21:3].). (He will proclaim: behold, I make all things new) ("And He who sits on the throne said, 'Behold, I am making all things new.' And He said*, 'Write, for these words are faithful and true'" [Rev. 21:5].). (We will see God face-to-face.) ("And He will wipe away every tear from their eyes; and there will no longer be *any* death; there will no longer be *any* mourning, or crying, or pain; the first things have passed away" [Rev. 22:4].). He will wipe away all our tears (Rev. 21:4). Death will be no more (Rev. 21:4). We will be given new names ("He who overcomes will inherit these things, and I will be his God and he will be My son" [Rev. 21:7].), [and we will exist as individual personalities encased in perfect bodies] ("Who will transform the body of our humble state into conformity with the body of His glory, by the exertion of the power that He has even to subject all things to Himself" [Phil. 3:21].). And we will grow eternally in knowledge and love of our infinite creator, honoring Him with our talent and gifts. Now I don't know about you, but I can get excited about that!

Jesus will be King of the earth from Mount Zion in Jerusalem. David, in his resurrected body, will be the king of Israel ("But they shall serve the LORD their God and David their king, whom I will raise up for them" [Jer. 30:9]. "And I, the LORD, will be their God, and My servant David will be prince among them; I the LORD have spoken" [Ezek. 34:24].), some of us in our resurrected bodies will be princes over nations. Jesus said, "I will put one of you in charge of five nations and another in charge of ten nations." Some of us will be judges, carrying out the law of God upon those who are living upon the earth in the flesh (which will be all Jews and Gentiles that live to the end of the tribulation who have accepted Jesus as Lord and Savior). Some of us will be administrators; do you know what most of us will be? Isaiah says over and over again most of us will be spiritual shepherds, because every person who goes into the millennium in the flesh will be babes in Christ. We, who are in our glorified bodies, will be the educational system of the world. And we will tutor them in the Word of God as their spiritual shepherds.

There is something missing, do you know what it is? There will not be any legislature. The Oklahoma legislature will cease to exist. The United States Congress will not be there. There will be no Supreme Court making decisions that are contrary to the Word of God. The Bible says that the law will go forth from Zion. There will be no political parties, no pressure groups that will try to lean on God and try to get Him to amend the law for their political philosophy. We are not going to have a wishy-washy wimp ruling the world who bows to political pressure. And we, in our glorified bodies, will administer that law, judge that law, and teach that law. And the result will be that the world will be flooded with righteousness as the waters cover the sea.

Does the Candidate Know That Many Evil Rulers and Terrorists Abroad Will Only Be Deterred from Violent Behavior through the Counter Threat of Force?

As a result of the fall of man in the Garden of Eden, our world is plagued with evil. Jeremiah lets us know of the severe evil in the heart of man. "The heart is more deceitful than all else and is desperately sick; who can understand it?" (Jer. 17:9). Will the candidate pursue a foreign policy of peace through military strength and not endanger our own national security? When a nation blessed by God turns its back on its Benefactor, God will place judgments upon the nation in order to call it to repentance. And one of those judgments can be that of giving the nation the kind of leaders it deserves. That is what He did with the Children of Israel and Judah. We will talk about that more in the last chapter.

Freedom is never free; it always cost something. The concept of peace through strength is nothing new. It has been around since the beginning of time. One of the reasons in the Old Testament, parents had so many children, particularly sons, was to demonstrate the appearance of strength. If you had a larger family than your neighbor, then your neighbor would think twice about attacking you or making you upset. Our Founding Fathers had a very similar belief system, and that makes sense since they took their philosophy from the Bible. It is impossible for a free people to remain free unless they stay strong from a martial perspective. George Washington once wrote, "To be prepared for war is one of the most effectual means of preserving peace….A free people ought not only be armed, but disciplined; to which end a uniform and well-digested plan is required." I agree with Washington. That is one of the reasons for our Second Amendment—the right to bear arms. In Washington's fifth annual address to Congress, he said,

> I cannot recommend to your notice measures for the fulfillment of our duties to the rest of the world, without again pressing upon you the necessity of placing ourselves in a condition of complete defense, and of exacting from them the fulfillment of their duties toward us.[19]

Washington wanted to prevent the European monarchs from trying to carve up the newly formed United States of America. As you will recall, the British still had troops stationed in America, and the Spanish still owned lands east of the Mississippi River. Washington was under no illusion that America's borders were secure. He continued to Congress:

> There is a rank due to the United States among nations, which will be withheld, if not absolutely lost, by the reputation of weakness. If we desire to avoid insult, we must be able to repel it; if we desire to secure peace, one of the most powerful instruments of our rising prosperity, it must be known that we are at all times ready for war.[20]

Samuel Adams said that it was our duty to our Creator to preserve our freedoms and unalienable rights of all Americans. Here is how he put it:

> It is the greatest absurdity to suppose it [would be] in the power of one, or any number of men, at the entering into society, to renounce their essential natural rights, or the means of preserving those rights; when the grand end of civil government, from the very nature of its institution, is for the support, protection, and defense of those very rights; the principal of which... are life, liberty, and property. If men, through fear, fraud, or mistake, should in terms renounce or give up any essential natural right, the eternal law of reason and the grand end of society would absolutely vacate such renunciation. The right to freedom being the gift of God Almighty, it is not in the power of man to alienate this gift and voluntarily become slaves.[21]

Adams later wrote friends in England and said, "It is the business of America to take care of herself; her situation, as you justly observe, depends upon her own virtue."

Benjamin Franklin, back in 1747, wrote about peace being the ultimate goal, but the way to achieve that goal was through strength. Here is what Franklin said:

> The very frame of our strength and readiness would be a means of discouraging our enemies; for 'tis a wise and true saying, that "One sword often keeps another in the scabbard." The way to secure peace is to be prepared for war. They that are on their guard, and appear ready to receive their adversaries, are in much less danger of being attacked than the supine, secure and negligent.[22]

Toward the end of Franklin's life, he felt the same:

> Our security lies, I think, in our growing strength, both in numbers and wealth; that creates an increasing ability of assisting this nation in its wars, which will make us more respectable, our friendship more valued, and our enmity feared; thence it will soon be thought proper to treat us not with justice only, but with kindness, and thence we may expect in a few years a total change of measures with regard to us; unless, by a neglect of military discipline, we should lose all martial spirit, and our western people become as tame as those in eastern dominions of Britain [India], when we may expect the same oppressions; for there

is much truth in the Italian saying, "Make yourselves sheep, and the wolves will eat you."[23]

Today we are threatened with the issue of terrorist who are hell-bent on eliminating the United States off the face of the earth. They refer to us as the Great Satan. That alone is a reason to be heavily armed to protect our nation. If terrorists ever get nuclear capacity, I have no doubt they would use them. I don't understand why other nations call terrorist *terrorist*; by our current administration, they have scrubbed the word out of the conversation. We need to be vigilant and not ignorant. We are warned in the Scriptures for us "to be wise as serpents but innocent as doves."

I don't think most people have any idea what the atomic age has introduced to the world. The atomic age began on July 16, 1945, when the first bomb was detonated at the Trinity Site at Alamogordo, New Mexico. President Truman told the world, "The basic power of the universe has been harnessed, the force from which the sun draws its power has been loosed." On August 6, 1945, the new weapon was used for the first time against the Japanese city of Hiroshima—three hundred thousand population. The bomb had a yield of 12.5 kilotons of TNT. That is a firecracker compared to the nuclear weapons we have today. It was detonated 1,900 feet above the city. By present day standards, it was a small bomb, yet that bomb, in a matter of a few seconds, killed eighty thousand people instantly, seventy thousand buildings were obliterated in Hiroshima.

It generated a firestorm that lasted for six hours that killed many thousands more. It produced a cyclone that came through the city and killed many thousands more; through radiation poisoning, a hundred thousand more died; seventy thousand were left.

Since Hiroshima, bombs have been tested, which are four thousand times as powerful as those dropped on Japan. Nuclear capacity has spread to many other countries. The standard nuclear bomb in today's arsenal has a yield of twenty megatons. Twenty megatons is 1,600 times the power of the bomb that was dropped on Hiroshima. One twenty–megaton bomb detonated over New York City could doom as many as thirty million people if the wind is blowing in the right direction. That is 10 percent of our population annihilated with one small bomb.

Israel hastily assembled thirteen atomic bombs during the Yon Kippur War of 1973. When it looked like they might lose the war, they put together thirteen bombs that they aimed at each of the Arab capitals. That was forty-two years ago; think what type of nuclear capacity that they would have now. Also, the commander and chief of the Israeli army said, "We no longer have a Masada complex. We will never march passively again; we will never kill ourselves rather than surrender. We have a Samson complex now." What that means is Israel may be annihilated, but they will take the rest of the Arab world with them.

When I was in school, I was taught that world peace would be guaranteed by what is called the balance of terror no one will ever push the button, because both sides will die. Winston Churchill said it was like two stinging scorpions in a box, they will just look at each other forever because they will never sting because to do so, both will die. They don't use that term anymore. Today, it is called mutually assured destruction. The acronym is MAD. There are two reasons why we are living on borrowed time when it comes to nuclear weapons. The first is it assumes there will never be an accident. The *Titanic* will not sink. Remember Three Mile Island, Chernobyl. Secondly, it assumes that man will always act rationally. What does Jeremiah say, "The heart is more deceitful than all else and is desperately sick; who can understand it?" (Jer. 17:9).

Civil defense is a total delusion. People say that we can build concrete bunkers. Nuclear bombs launched from subs will arrive in this country in seven minutes. Do you know that it takes fifteen minutes to activate the US civil defense warning system? So eight minutes after you are dead, you get the warning that you need to go to your shelter. But the pink elephant in the room is we don't have bunkers for the population to hide in anyway.

I don't think the average Christian knows what happens with a nuclear explosion. Nicholas Wade, in his book *A World Beyond Healing*, gives us a graphic picture of a nuclear explosion.

The explosion of a nuclear weapon is an event of immense power...Within a fraction of a millionth of a second, the nuclear materials and casing of a one megaton weapon are transformed into a packet of energy five times hotter than the center of the sun. Out of this mini-sun bursts a flash of X-rays so intense that the air for several feet around the weapon is heated into an incandescent ball. This little fireball, only a few millionths of a second old, contains the vaporized contents of the weapon, and a vast flux of energy created by the fission and fusion reactions of the nuclear explosion. So immense an amount of energy packed into a tiny space creates temperatures of 100 million degrees centigrade and pressures of millions of pounds per square inch. A violent explosion begins. In less than a thousandth of a second, the fireball of a one-megaton weapon has grown to 440 feet across. In ten seconds, the fireball is more than a mile in diameter.[24]

The latest studies all testify to the fact that the words of Matthew 24 can become literally true.

Jonathan Schell's book, *The Fate of the Earth*, has a very alarming sentence. He is not a believer, and here is what he says about our knowledge of nuclear weapons. His quote has been modified as Scriptures are placed in what he says will happen.

The following judgment can now be made barring in mind that the possible consequences of the detonation of thousands of megatons of nuclear explosives include the blinding of all insects, birds, beast all over the world; the extinction of many ocean species many of which are at the base of the food chain, [Rev. 16:3: And every living creature in the sea died] the temporary or permanent alteration of the climate on the globe, the pollution of the whole ecosphere with oxides of nitrogen destroying the ozone layer, [Rev. 8:12: And a third of the sun was struck, a third of the moon, and a third of the stars, so that a third of them were darkened. A third of the day did not shine, and likewise the night] the incapacitation of unprotected people who go out into the sunlight, the blinding of people who go out into the sunlight, a significant decrease in photosynthesis in plants around the world, the scalding and killing of crops, [Rev. 8:7: And a third of the trees were burned up, and all green grass was burned up] increases in the rate of cancer and mutations around the world, [Rev. 16:2: And a foul and loathsome sore came upon the men who had the mark of the beast] global epidemics, [Luke 21:11: And there will be great earthquakes in various places, and famine and pestilences] the possible poisoning of all vertebrates by sharply increased levels of vitamin D in their skin as a result of increased ultraviolet light, [Rev. 16:8: The fourth angel poured out his bowl on the sun, and power was given to him to scorch men with fire, and men were scorched with great heat] and the outright slaughter on targeted countries of most human beings, and other living things by the initial nuclear radiation, the fireballs, the thermo pulses, the blast waves, the mass fires, and the fallout from the explosion, [Rev. 9:18: By these three plagues a third of mankind was killed, by the fire and the smoke and the brimstone] and considering that these consequences will all interact with one another in unguessable ways, and further more are all in likelihood an incomplete list which will be added to as our knowledge of earth increases, one must conclude that a full scale nuclear holocaust could lead to the extinction of mankind." [Matt. 24:22: And unless those days were shortened, no flesh would be saved; but for the sake of the elect, those days will be shortened].[25]

And that is all one sentence. The day of Armageddon had arrived; mankind is teetering on the verge of extinction. And man's answer is disarmament. I want to tell you something: disarmament is pie in the sky. It will never be realized because it flies in the face of mankind. Furthermore, even if—presto—we could rid ourselves of all the nuclear arms, we could never rid ourselves of the knowledge of how to make them. I will guarantee you that when a war breaks out, the nations will do exactly what we did in WWII. They will assemble nuclear bombs as fast as they can to make sure that they win the war. The knowledge and capacity to produce nuclear weapons would still exist, and what man has made, he has always used. There is only one hope for mankind, and that is Jesus Christ. Thank God He is coming soon!

Does the Candidate Know
That God Is Not a Socialist?

It is important that we realize that Jesus was not a socialist. To hear some Christians talk, you would think that the Gospel is a socialist manifesto. I want to start with the parable of the talents found in Matthew 35:14–30 to start this discussion.

"For *it is* just like a man *about* to go on a journey, who called his own slaves and entrusted his possessions to them. To one he gave five talents, to another, two, and to another, one, each according to his own ability; and he went on his journey." Don't miss that. It would have been irresponsible for God to have given the third servant five or two talents because he would have squandered the talents. Never get upset because somebody else has been given more by God than you have been given. Let me tell you why. God is only going to hold you accountable for what He gave you. He is not holding you accountable for what he gave somebody else. If we were more grateful with what He gave us, we would not be so upset about what is happening with the Joneses. God gave them based upon their own abilities. Let us keep reading. "Immediately the one who had received the five talents went and traded with them, and gained five more talents. In the same manner the one who *had received* the two *talents* gained two more. But he who received the one *talent* went away, and dug *a hole* in the ground and hid his master's money." God expects you to take what He gives you and to maximize its potential.

> Now after a long time the master of those slaves came* and settled* accounts with them. The one who had received the five talents came up and brought five more talents, saying, "Master, you entrusted five talents to me. See, I have gained five more talents." His master said to him, "Well done, good and faithful slave. You were faithful with a few things, I will put you in charge of many things; enter into the joy of your master." Also the one who *had received* the two talents came up and said, "Master, you entrusted two talents to me. See, I have gained two more talents." His master said to him, "Well done, good and faithful slave. You were faithful with a few things, I will put you in charge of many things; enter into the joy of your master."[26]

Please note that the statement "Well done good and faithful servant" is in reference to how people handle money. We use it to accommodate other areas, but the context is monetary considerations. "And the one also who had received the one talent came up and said, 'Master, I knew you to be a hard man, reaping where you did not sow and gathering where you scattered no *seed*. And I was afraid, and went away and hid your talent in the ground. See, you have what is yours.'" (The servant says, "It is too big of a risk, I might have lost it. So I did not do anything with it.") "But his master answered and said to him, 'You wicked, lazy slave, you knew that I reap where I did not sow and gather where I scattered no *seed*.'" (He says, "Yes, I am a hard man, and you ought to take me seriously. I have entrusted things to your care. Don't play with them, you wicked lazy slave.") "Then you ought to have put my money in the bank, and on my arrival I would have received my *money* back with interest." (Again, God expects us to be productive and to increase our talents with the bare minimum of at least interest.) "Therefore take away the talent from him, and give it to the one who has the ten talents." (Now here is the principle.) "For to everyone who has, *more* shall be given, and he will have an abundance; but from the one who does not have, even what he does have shall be taken away. Throw out the worthless slave into the outer darkness; in that place there will be weeping and gnashing of teeth."

That certainly does not sound like socialism. Notice that it is redistribution of wealth but in the opposite direction. God is taking from those who have less and giving it to those who have more, or, more accurately, God is taking from those who are unproductive and giving it to those who are productive. The redistribution of wealth that is going on in our society today is completely backward. God rewards those who are productive and does not punish their productivity. God also punished the unproductive servant due to his "laziness" as Jesus describes their lack of productivity.

Paul declares that we have something to look forward to in Romans 8:18. "For I consider that the sufferings of this present time are not worthy to be compared with the glory that is to be revealed to us." Paul reiterates this in 1 Corinthians 2:9. "But just as it is written, 'Things which eye has not seen and ear has not heard, And *which* have not entered the heart of man, All that God has prepared for those who love Him.'" Even Jesus tells us that He has rewards for those who are his children. "Behold, I am coming quickly, and My reward *is* with Me, to render to every man according to what he has done. I am the Alpha and the Omega, the first and the last, the beginning and the end. Blessed are those who wash their robes, so that they may have the right to the tree of life, and may enter by the gates into the city" (Rev. 22:12–14). The point is simply that there are rewards for believers in Christ. There are some general rewards for all believers, but then there are many more rewards that are for a specific purpose. These rewards are for all those who accept Jesus as their personal Lord and Savior.

General Rewards for All Believers

The Judgment Seat of God

The most significant reward for all believers is salvation in Jesus Christ. "For God so loved the world, that He gave His only begotten Son, that whoever believes in Him shall not perish, but have eternal life" (John 3:16). Eternal life comes through Jesus Christ; in fact, Jesus states this point blank. "Jesus said to him, 'I am the way, and the truth, and the life; no one comes to the Father but through Me'" (John 14:6). Jesus tells us that He is the only way to the Father. Salvation is for all who go through Jesus, and apart from Him, there is no possible way to obtain salvation. Paul lets us know that it is through the grace of God that the gift of salvation is given to us. "For by grace you have been saved through faith; and that not of yourselves, *it is* the gift of God; not as a result of works, so that no one may boast" (Eph. 2:8–9). Salvation is for all believers in Christ Jesus. That is the first and most significant of rewards.

Another promise or reward for Christians is the rapture of the church. The Apostle Paul saw the rapture as a motivational factor for him to continue his work on the earth. "I press on toward the goal for the prize of the upward call of God in Christ Jesus" (Phil. 2:14). There are many people that do not believe that there is going to be a rapture. Many people say that the term *rapture* is not a biblical word. The word *rapture* is a Latin word that means "to snatch out," "to take away," "to take out of." You will find the word *rapture* in the Latin Vulgate, the oldest translation of the Bible. After all, a word does not have to be in English for it to be a biblical word. "People shall be caught up to meet Jesus in the sky (1 Thess. 4:17), the Latin says *rapamere*, which is a declension of the Latin word *raptus*. We use it because it is easier to say "rapture" when we bring the concept into English. To express it in English, you have to use two or more words.

The rapture is not mentioned in the Old Testament because it is a promise to the church. In the New Testament, the concept is mentioned in 1 Thessalonians.

> But we do not want you to be uninformed, brethren, about those who are asleep, so that you will not grieve as do the rest who have no hope. For if we believe that Jesus died and rose again, even so God will bring with Him those who have fallen asleep in Jesus. For this we say to you by the word of the Lord, that we who are alive and remain until the coming of the Lord, will not precede those who have fallen asleep. For the Lord Himself will descend from heaven with a shout, with the voice of *the* archangel and with the trumpet of God, and the dead in Christ will rise first. Then we who are alive and remain will be caught up together with them in the clouds to meet the Lord in the air, and so we shall always be with the Lord. Therefore comfort one another with these words.[27] (1 Thess. 4:13–18)

The rapture is to be a source of comfort to Christians. Jesus will appear in the sky. The dead in Christ will be resurrected and will meet Him in the sky. Then those who are alive will be translated and will also meet Jesus in the sky. When Jesus comes, He will come down from heaven, and there will be the sound of a trumpet. At that point, the living and the dead shall be caught up to meet Jesus in the clouds.

Glorification is another reward for the believer. The Apostle Paul says in Philippians 3:20–21 that we will receive new glorified bodies that cannot sin.

> For our citizenship is in heaven, from which also we eagerly wait for a Savior, the Lord Jesus Christ; who will transform the body of our humble state into conformity with the body of His glory, by the exertion of the power that He has even to subject all things to Himself.[28]

1 John 3:2 lets us know that our bodies will be just like Christ's body after the resurrection. "Beloved, now we are children of God, and it has not appeared as yet what we will be. We know that when He appears, we will be like Him, because we will see Him just as He is." This lets us know that we will have bodies that are immortal and are perfected. We will have a body that cannot sin and will not suffer decay in any way.

Sanctification is another reward that all believers will receive. In fact, sanctification is a process that is ongoing in this life. Part of God's purpose is to conform us to the image of His son Jesus Christ.

> For those whom He foreknew, He also predestined
> *to become* conformed to the image of His Son, so that
> He would be the firstborn among many brethren; and
> these whom He predestined, He also called; and these
> whom He called, He also justified; and these whom
> He justified, He also glorified.[29] (Rom. 8:29–30)

The sanctification process begins when we accept Jesus
Christ as our Savior and as our Lord and is not complete
until we pass into eternity.

There are other rewards that we will receive when we
arrived at the throne of God. Look at these powerful words
from the book of Jude 24–25: "Now to Him who is able
to keep you from stumbling, and to make you stand in the
presence of His glory blameless with great joy, to the only
God our Savior, through Jesus Christ our Lord, *be* glory,
majesty, dominion and authority, before all time and now
and forever. Amen." It is God who enables us to be able to
stand in the presence of the Almighty. But please notice
that we will be presented blameless and with great joy and
rejoicing in His presence.

One of my personal favorites is that Jesus will present
me before the Father and confess me to Him. "Therefore
everyone who confesses Me before men, I will also confess
him before My Father who is in heaven" (Matt. 10:32). Do
you know what that means? That means there is going to
come a day when I will stand before the throne room of
God, and Jesus will come stand by my side, He will give

me a warm embrace. He will turn to His Father, God, and say, "Dad, this is James, he is My brother. He confessed Me before men." That gives me chills to know that day will soon be coming for me. But not just for me but for all those who made Jesus their personal Lord and Savior.

Another reward is that we will get to see God face-to-face. "Blessed are the pure in heart, for they shall see God" (Matt. 5:8). You will recall in Exodus 33:20 that God tells Moses no man can see his face and live. "But He said, 'You cannot see My face, for no man can see Me and live!'" But for the believer, we will be able to have the privilege of seeing God face-to-face. What a wonderful blessing and reward to receive.

In 1 Peter 5:10, it lets us know that God will perfect, confirm, strengthen, and establish us in Christ Jesus. "The God of all grace, who called you to His eternal glory in Christ, will Himself perfect, confirm, strengthen *and* establish you." What a glorious promise to receive from Christ.

One final promise I want to mention as we stand before the throne of God is, we will be formally adopted as sons and daughters, and our bodies will be redeemed. "And not only this, but also we ourselves, having the first fruits of the Spirit, even we ourselves groan within ourselves, waiting eagerly for *our* adoption as sons, the redemption of our body" (Rom. 8:23).

General Rewards for All Believers

The Judgment Seat of Christ

There are promises that we will have when we stand before the judgment seat of Christ. This judgment is different than what you are thinking. This judgment is to determine our degree of rewards in heaven, not our salvation. Our salvation has already been established in Jesus Christ. In Revelation 3:5, our names are in the book of life. Halleluiah! "He who overcomes will thus be clothed in white garments; and I will not erase his name from the book of life, and I will confess his name before My Father and before His angels."

The Apostle Paul once said that he was the chief of all sinners. I think he has some competition with me because I am a sinner saved by the grace of God. I thank God for this next reward at the seat of Christ, and that is God will remember my sins no more. "For I will be merciful to their iniquities, And I will remember their sins no more" (Heb. 8:12). My sins were nailed to the cross over two thousand years ago when Jesus was crucified. The book of Colossians gives us a very vivid picture of Christ nailing our sins to the cross. "When you were dead in your transgressions and the uncircumcision of your flesh, He made you alive together with Him, having forgiven us all our transgressions, having canceled out the certificate of debt consisting of decrees against us [In those days, the certificate of debt was the list of offenses that the criminal was convicted of.], which was hostile to us; and He has taken it out of the way, having nailed it to the cross" (Col. 2:13–15). When Jesus was crucified on the cross, He took my sins and nailed them to the cross. It is as if Satan gave Jesus a sheet of paper with all my sins listed on them. In reality, that was just the Table of Contents. Jesus took the sheet and washed it with His blood and then handed Satan a blank sheet of paper because my sins were covered by His blood. "When He had disarmed the rulers and authorities, He made a public display of them, having triumphed over them through Him." That is enough to make you want to jump up and dance.

Not only are our sins forgiven, they are also forgotten. "Truly, truly, I say to you, he who hears My word, and believes Him who sent Me, has eternal life, and does not come into judgment, but has passed out of death into life" (John 5:25). I thank God that I will never stand before God and have to give account for my sins. They were covered on the cross. God says that we are going to be held accountable to Him on judgment day for at least five things. There will come a day when every single person will stand before God. When we stand before God, do you know who will be present? Every person who has ever walked the face of the earth will be present. Your parents, Adolph Hitler, Attila the Hun, Jeffery Dahmer, Martin Luther King Jr., Nero Caesar, Saddam Hussein, Christopher Columbus, Geronimo will all be present. Everyone who has ever lived on the face of the earth will be there on that day.

On that day, I will know everything about you, and you will know everything about me. That may make you feel a little uncomfortable. We are going to be standing in heaven, and you are going to see this, hear this, and experience this. And God is going to say, "James Taylor, come on down, you're the next contestant on…no, not really." And I am going to be standing before the throne of God. And somehow, I don't know how he is going to do it. He is going to show all five of these areas.

Let me say, that as a Christian, I thank God I will never stand before Him and be judged of my sins. That is what the cross is all about. God is only going to remember the good things. Hebrews 6:10 reveals that to us. "For God is not unjust so as to forget your work and the love which you have shown toward His name, in having ministered and in still ministering to the saints." Let me also say for everyone who is a Christian this has nothing to do with you entering heaven. It has to do with your degrees of rewards.

First, we are going to be responsible to God for every thought. "We are casting down imagination, and every high thing that exalts itself against the knowledge of God, and bringing into captivity every thought to the obedience of Christ" (2 Cor. 10:5). We have the capability as Christians to bring every thought to obedience to Christ. Think about your thoughts, good or bad, and they are accountable.

Second, we will give account for every word. "But I tell you that every careless word that people speak, they shall give an accounting for it in the Day of Judgment. For by your words you will be justified and by your words you will be condemned" (Matt. 12:36–37). You think about the words you have said to one another, your significant other, your parents, your children, church leaders. God says, good or bad, every word we will give account.

Third, we will give account for every action (deed). "For we must all appear before the judgment seat of Christ, so that each one may be recompensed for his deeds in the body, according to what he has done, whether good or bad" (2 Cor. 5:10).

Fourth, we will give account for every attitude. This is one you probably didn't think about. "The heart is more deceitful than all else and is desperately sick; who can understand it? I the Lord search the heart; I test the mind, even to give to each man according to his ways, according to the results of his deeds" (Jer. 17:9–10).

Fifth, we will give account for every motive. "Therefore do not go on passing judgment before the time, *but wait* until the Lord comes who will both bring to light the things hidden in the darkness and disclose the motives of *men's* hearts; and then each man's praise will come to him from God" (1 Cor. 4:5).

The Queen of England often visits Bob Morrow Castle. On one occasion, when she was walking by herself, it started to rain. She rushed to the shelter of the nearest cottage. A lady came to the door, who was really upset that someone would bother her at that time in the morning. She opened the door a few inches and barked, "What do you want?"

The Queen didn't introduce herself. She merely asked, "May I borrow an umbrella?"

"Just a minute," grumbled the woman. She slammed the door, was gone for a moment, and returned, bringing the rattiest umbrella she could find, one with broken ribs and small holes. She pushed it through the door and said, "Here." The Queen of England thanked her and went on her way with the ragged umbrella.

The next morning, the queen's full escort, dressed in full uniform, pulled up in front of the cottage. One of the escorts knocked on the door and returned the umbrella to the woman, saying, "Madam, the Queen of England thanks you." As he walked away, he heard her mutter, "If I'd only known, I'd have given her my best."

Someday, we will all stand before the King of heaven, and I believe we will be hearing some Christians who will be muttering, "If I'd only known, I'd have given You my best." The fact is, we do know, and yet many of us still give Christ the scraps, the leftovers, whatever costs us the least. Because God loved us, He gave us His best, his Son. Can we give Him anything less than our best? There are many people who life has not been too kind for them, and they toil throughout their lives. One of the other benefits is God will give us rest from our toils. "Come to Me, all who are weary and heavy-laden, and I will give you rest" (Matt. 11:28).

One final benefit that I want to mention is we will have full understanding of the mysteries of God and acknowledged as belonging to the Father and New Jerusalem. "For now we see in a mirror dimly, but then face to face; now I know in part, but then I will know fully just as I also have been fully known" (1 Cor. 13:12). I look forward to understanding the mysteries of God. These are some of the general rewards that all believers receive from the Lord. This is not an exhaustive list but just to get you to understand there are some things every believer receives. However, there are many that are specialized rewards. Those were the general rewards for all those who have accepted Jesus Christ as their personal Lord and Savior.

Specialized Rewards

When we look at the specialized rewards, you will only receive these if you do these things and act in the appropriate manner. There is no socialism in these items. I want to start with the beatitudes. "He [Jesus] opened His mouth and *began* to teach them, saying, 'Blessed are the poor in spirit, for theirs is the kingdom of heaven'" (Matt. 5:2–12). Poor in spirit means to be humble, to have a correct estimate of oneself. "For through the grace given to me I say to everyone among you not to think more highly of himself than he ought to think; but to think so as to have sound judgment, as God has allotted to each a measure of faith" (Rom. 12:3). It does not mean to be "poor spirited" and have no backbone at all! "Poor in Spirit" is the opposite of the world's attitude of self-praise. It is also not a false humility that says, "I am not worth anything, I can't do anything." It is honesty with ourselves: we know ourselves, accept ourselves, and try to be ourselves to the glory of God.

> Blessed are those who mourn, for they shall be comforted. Blessed are the gentle, for they shall inherit the earth. Blessed are those who hunger and thirst for righteousness, for they shall be satisfied. Blessed are the merciful, for they shall receive mercy. Blessed are the pure in heart, for they shall see God. Blessed are the peacemakers, for they shall be called sons of God. Blessed are those who have been persecuted for the sake of righteousness, for theirs is the kingdom of heaven. Blessed are you when *people* insult you and persecute you, and falsely say all kinds of evil against you because of Me. Rejoice and be glad, for your reward in heaven is great; for in the same way they persecuted the prophets who were before you.[30] (Matt. 5:4–12)

If you do not possess these qualities in your life, you will miss out on the blessings as a Christian. These rewards are very specific to those who possessed the qualities listed.

The sacrifices that you have given will be returned up to a hundredfold. "Other *seeds* fell into the good soil, and as they grew up and increased, they yielded a crop and produced thirty, sixty, and a hundredfold" (Mark 4:8). Some people have the gift of giving, and they shall be rewarded. If a person is sold out to Jesus Christ, you do not have to beg them to tithe to the Lord or beg them to serve in church or beg them to attend church; they eagerly desire to do those things. God says He will reward them for their efforts.

Another specialized reward is the humble will be exalted. "Humble yourselves in the presence of the Lord, and He will exalt you" (James 4:10). If you are not a humble person, there will be no exalting you by the Lord.

When Paul writes to Timothy from Rome, he commends Christians for their service to the Church.

> The Lord grant mercy to the house of Onesiphorus, for he often refreshed me and was not ashamed of my chains; but when he was in Rome, he eagerly searched for me and found me—the Lord grant to him to find mercy from the Lord on that day—and you know very well what services he rendered at Ephesus.[31] (2 Tim. 2:16–18)

There is a specialized reward for those who have practiced self-control in this life.

> Do you not know that those who run in a race all run, but *only* one receives the prize? Run in such a way that you may win. Everyone who competes in the games exercises self-control in all things. They then *do it* to

> receive a perishable wreath, but we an imperishable.
> Therefore I run in such a way, as not without aim; I box
> in such a way, as not beating the air; but I discipline
> my body and make it my slave, so that, after I have
> preached to others, I myself will not be disqualified.[32]
> (1 Cor. 9:24–27)

There is a crown of exaltation for those who are soul winners. Paul makes reference to the Thessalonians as part of his crown. "For who is our hope or joy or crown of exultation? Is it not even you, in the presence of our Lord Jesus at His coming?" (1 Thess. 2:19).

There is a special reward for those who have loved the appearance of Christ. "In the future there is laid up for me the crown of righteousness, which the Lord, the righteous Judge, will award to me on that day; and not only to me, but also to all who have loved His appearing" (2 Tim. 4:8). One of the great subjects in the Word of God is eschatology—the study of end-times events. For those who love the appearance of Christ and His return, they will have a special reward.

There are people who have endured unbelievable trials in life. James lets us know that they will receive the Crown of Life. "Blessed is a man who perseveres under trial; for once he has been approved, he will receive the crown of life which *the Lord* has promised to those who love Him" (James 1:12).

There is a special reward for faithful elders who serve their church with an unfading crown of glory.

> Therefore, I exhort the elders among you, as *your* fellow elder and witness of the sufferings of Christ, and a partaker also of the glory that is to be revealed, shepherd the flock of God among you, exercising oversight not under compulsion, but voluntarily, according to *the will of* God; and not for sordid gain, but with eagerness; nor yet as lording it over those allotted to your charge, but proving to be examples to the flock. And when the Chief Shepherd appears, you will receive the unfading crown of glory. You younger men, likewise, be subject to *your* elders; and all of you, clothe yourselves with humility toward one another, for God is opposed to the proud, but gives grace to the humble.[33] (1 Pet. 5:1–4)

I could go on but this gives you the idea. There are certain rewards that every believer will receive, but there are a lot more that are specialized. If you are not an elder in a church, then you will not be blessed with the unfading crown of glory. If you have not endured through trials and remained faithful, you will not receive the crown of life. If you are not a soul winner, do not expect the crown of exaltation. One of the blessings of eternity is that we will not be jealous of someone else's rewards. We will be happy we are there. I think the only regret is that we didn't do more for Christ while we had the opportunity. God is not a socialist and never will be. God sees us as individuals with gifts that are to be used for His kingdom. He is the rewarder of our lives to everyone who accepts Christ, but not everybody gets the same rewards.

6

The Answer to Our Problems Is Found in God's Word

"For *it is* time for judgment to begin with the household of God; and if *it begins* with us first, what *will be* the outcome for those who do not obey the gospel of God?" (1 Pet. 4:17). Repentance starts with the household of God. That means that God holds the church responsible for what is happening in our nation. There is one passage of Scripture that everyone turns to when it comes to our union, and that is 2 Chronicles 7:14. But one must look at all of God's Word to get an accurate picture of where we are and things to come. "If My people [Who are God's people? That would be both the Jews first and the Christian second] who are called by My name humble themselves and pray and seek My face and turn from their wicked ways, then I will hear from heaven, will forgive their sin and will heal their land" (2 Chron. 7:14). Our land is in trouble because the body of Christ is a sleeping giant. The only answer is repentance, and even that might not be enough.

Most people know the story of Jonah, and if I were to ask you what is the first thing that comes to your mind? You would probably say whale. That is too bad because the Bible does not say anything about a whale; the book of Jonah is a book about God. Jonah is a prophet, and God tells him to go to Nineveh. Nineveh was the capitol of Assyria. Assyria was located 550 miles northeast of Israel. But Jonah decides he had to go to Tarshish, which is 2,500 miles to the northwest. Jonah is a renegade preacher who does not want to do what God called him to do.

After Jonah goes on the first submarine ride in history, he agrees to do what God asked him to do. Jonah goes to Nineveh and preaches to the city, and in one day, the entire city repents. Jonah is the world's greatest evangelist. Nobody has been able to do what Jonah has been able to do and that is to get an entire city to repent. In fact, according to the Scripture, not only did he get the people to repent, but even the animals put on the appearance of repentance with sackcloth and ashes.

> Then the people of Nineveh believed in God; and they called a fast and put on sackcloth from the greatest to the least of them. When the word reached the king of Nineveh, he arose from his throne, laid aside his robe from him, covered *himself* with sackcloth and sat on the ashes. He issued a proclamation and it said, "In Nineveh by the decree of the king and his nobles: Do not let man, beast, herd, or flock taste a thing. Do

not let them eat or drink water. But both man and
beast must be covered with sackcloth; and let men call
on God earnestly that each may turn from his wicked
way and from the violence which is in his hands.
Who knows, God may turn and relent and withdraw
His burning anger so that we will not perish."[1] (Jon.
3:5–9)

The king said to let the entire nation repent, and he said
to let the animals get saved too. We are talking about serious
repentance. Now animals can't get saved, but the point was
that they were so repentant that they even applied the acts
of repentance to the animals. They wanted that when God
looked down in those forty days, that the animals would be
saying they accept God. That is some serious repentance.

I want you to notice something about the people of
Nineveh. Conversion changed the political environment
of Nineveh. It didn't happen because they made better
laws, hired more policemen, or provided more arms for the
people to reduce the violence. The violence got removed
because the people met a living God. The thing that
changes people and brings about peace to an environment
is when men repent before a living God. Because then, men
are changed from the inside; their hearts were different.
Nineveh still had the same king, the same congress, and
the same city council. The difference now was there was
a heart transformation, and that translated into actions
and behavior. That is the only thing that will help America

change, and that is for the people of America to encounter the living God, who has the power to transform our hearts. It really doesn't matter who is in public office; it matters if their hearts are committed to the living God.

The Rev. James A. Garfield (1831–1881) said this:

> The people are responsible for the character of the Congress. If that body be ignorant, reckless, and corrupt, it is because the people tolerated ignorance, recklessness, and corruption. If it be intelligent, brave, and pure, it is because the people demand these high qualities to represent them in the national legislature. If the next centennial does not find us a great nation... It will be because those who represent the enterprise, the culture, and the morality of the nation do not aid in controlling the political forces.[2]

The Rev. James A. Garfield was also the twentieth president of the United States of America. We are responsible for our leaders by what we tolerate. This is why what we support we get the benefit of it or the curse of it. That is why we must evaluate who the candidates are that we are supporting. How we vote means we get their good or their bad, depending upon their influence on society. Remember, the Apostle John lets us know that what we support, good or bad, we get that blessing or curse. That is certainly true about how we vote.

There are two nations that have began based on God Almighty: the nation of Israel and the United States of

America. The nation of Israel began to turn their backs on God, and they split into the ten northern tribes of Israel and the two southern tribes of Judah. When you read the Bible, after the nation split, the northern tribe of Israel never had a righteous king. You read the words, "And he did evil in the sight of the Lord," referring to the kings. Not one righteous king was found in Israel when the kingdom divided. Israel left the sound principles of the Lord, and God removed Israel from His sight. Judah lasted a little over one hundred years longer, but eventually, God removed them as well.

America is analogous to the nation of Israel. As Israel was obedient to God, He blessed them; as they were disobedient, He cursed them. In 2 Kings 23, the nation of Israel has already been removed, and Judah was left. By this time, they were doing unspeakable sins. They had temple prostitutes, they set up phallic symbols in the temple, and they were even burning their children alive to the false god, Moloch. The most righteous king was Josiah (the boy king who came to power at the age of eight), who led the nation in repentance, and he got rid of all the sin. He had to undo many of the things that his grandfather had done as king. Let us look at some of the things Manasseh did as king.

"Manasseh was twelve years old when he became king" (2 Kings 21:1). That's a young age to become king. Manasseh actually co-ruled with his father, Hezekiah. It was a mentorship. But when Hezekiah died, Manasseh had the whole kingdom.

"And he reigned 55 years in Jerusalem" (2 Kings 21:1). That's a long time in office by anybody's standards. No term limits, so they were stuck. He had an unbelievable influence for over half a century in the nation. If you really work at it, you can do a fair amount of damage in fifty-five years. For that matter, you can do a fair amount of damage in just four years. Imagine having a corrupt, immoral, God-hating, Christian-hating president over the United States of America from 1960 until the year 2015.

"And he did evil in the sight of the Lord, according to the abominations of the nations whom the Lord disposed before the sons of Israel" (2 Kings 21:2). And he did the kind of evil that was in the Promised Land before Joshua arrived to wipe out the Canaanites as God commanded. Sexual perversion and child sacrifice were everyday stuff among these people. "According to the abominations of the nations" means that as perverse and violent that the Canaanites were, they had nothing on Manasseh. He equaled their perversion. "For he rebuilt the high places which Hezekiah his father had destroyed" (2 Kings 21:3a). The high places were places on top of hills that were for religious ceremonies. They were not worshipping God.

"And he erected altar's for Baal and made an Asherah, as Ahab king of Israel had done, and worshipped all the hosts of heaven and served them" (2 Kings 21:3b). Manasseh wouldn't allow the worship of God. He probably fought to keep the Ten Commandments from being posted on the schools' walls. He believed in religious diversity and accommodated the worship of any pagan religion. Baal was one of the king's favorite. Asherah was right up there too. An Asherah was a wooden symbol of female deity. They were huge phallic symbols closely aligned with the worship of sex.

"And he built altars in the house of the Lord, of which the Lord had said, 'In Jerusalem I will put my Name.' For he built altars for all the hosts of heaven in the two courts of the house of the Lord" (2 Kings 21:4–5). Catch this. Solomon built the temple in Jerusalem so that God might have a place so His presence could dwell, and the people could come and worship. Manasseh's heart had become so corrupt that he actually went into the holy place and set up altars of worship for these repulsive, imported gods. That was bad enough, but it gets worse.

"And he made his son pass through the fire" (2 Kings 21:6a). One of the gods of Manasseh was Moloch. They set up a huge statue similar to Buddha. They would stoke the fires until the iron image was made white-hot. The hands of this god were stretched out palms opened. As people worshipped and worked themselves into a frenzy, they would take their firstborn sons and toss the child to his death in those white-hot hands. Can you believe this guy? But we are not quite through with Manasseh's résumé.

"He practiced witchcraft and used divination, and dealt with mediums and spiritists. He did much evil in the sight of the Lord provoking Him to anger" (2 Kings 21:6b). The original language gives the impression that he not only dealt with these masters of the occult, but he placed them in positions of leadership in the country. In essence, he named witches and warlocks to his cabinet. But he wasn't through yet.

"Then he set the carved image of the Asherah that he had made, in the house of which the Lord said to David and to his son Solomon, 'In this house and in Jerusalem, which I have chosen from all the tribes of Israel, I will put My name forever.' But they did not listen, and Manasseh seduced them to do evil more than the nations whom the Lord destroyed before the sons of Israel" (2 Kings 21:7). He actually had the gall to drag this massive phallic symbol and place it in God's temple. Do you see how far down the tubes this guy has gone? Remember, this was a man with a godly heritage. His father, Hezekiah, was one of the few righteous kings of Judah. He knew better. But he deliberately turned his back on God. Now God does not let this kind of thing go unchecked. We make choices, and God responds. Fifty-five years may seem like a lot of rope to us, but eventually, Manasseh came to the end of that rope. God has a clear word for the renegade king of Judah.

> Now the Lord spoke through His servants the prophets, saying, "Because Manasseh king of Judah has done these abominations, having done wickedly more than all the Amorites did who were before him,

and has also made Judah sin with his idols;" therefore thus says the Lord the God of Israel, "Behold I am bringing such calamity on Jerusalem and Judah, that whoever hears of it, both his ears shall tingle, and I will stretch over Jerusalem the line of Samaria and the plummet of the house of Ahab." (2 Kings 21:10–13)

In other words, judgment day had arrived. Did you catch the phrase, "Manasseh did more than all the Amorites who were before him"? Earlier, the Scripture says he equaled their sin and perversion. Now he had passed them. This guy was doing stuff they never thought of doing. And he was doing it in God's special city, Jerusalem.

"And I will stretch over Jerusalem the line of Samaria and the plummet of the house of Ahab" (2 Kings 21:13a) [terms used by survey crews]. When you have a hill that you want to level, you first call the surveyors in with their plummet, or level. God is saying to Manasseh's sins, "I'm going to come into Jerusalem, and I am going to level it." And just in case that metaphor didn't sink in, God used another one.

"And I will wipe Jerusalem as one wipes a dish, wiping it and turning it upside down" (2 Kings 21:13b). When you dry the dishes, how do you do it? Usually you take the dish in your hand, dry one side, then turn it over and dry the other side so that every bit of moisture is wiped away. God is saying, "That is what I am going to do in response to Manasseh's sin. I'm going to wipe Jerusalem clean."

"Moreover Manasseh shed very much innocent blood until he had filled Jerusalem from one end to another; besides his sin with which he made Judah sin, in doing evil in the sight of the Lord" (2 Kings 21:16). Tradition tells us it was Manasseh who took the prophet Isaiah, put him in a hollowed-out log, and sawed him in half (Heb. 11:37). Why? Because he did not want to hear the voice of God, and he tried to silence Him. The next verses record his obituary: "Now the rest of the acts of Manasseh and all that he had did and his sin which he committed, are they not written in the Book of the Chronicles of the Kings of Judah? And Manasseh slept with his fathers and was buried in the garden of his own house, in the garden of Uzza, and Amon his son became king in his place" (2 Kings 21:17–18).

Manasseh did much evil in the sight of God. I tell you what he did because that is important in the judgment that is to come. Remember, Josiah cleaned up Judah and removed all the evil in the land. He was a good king who did right in the eyes of the Lord. We must take heed of 2 Kings 23:26–27 because I think this passage takes priority over 2 Chronicles 7:14.

> However, the LORD did not turn from the fierceness of His great wrath with which His anger burned against Judah, because of all the provocations with which Manasseh had provoked Him. The LORD said, "I will remove Judah also from My sight, as I have

> removed Israel. And I will cast off Jerusalem, this city
> which I have chosen, and the temple of which I said,
> 'My name shall be there.'"[3] (2 Kings 23:26–27)

God was true to His word and removed Judah as He said; however, He did not do it during the life of King Josiah. God waited until Josiah had died, and God did it when his son was in office.

Let me connect the dots as we come to a close. Today we kill four thousand babies a day in the name of freedom of choice for women. One of the ways we do that is by injecting a saline solution into the womb. As the baby breathes, it ingests the solution, and it burns it on the inside and on the outside. After about twenty-four to seventy-two hours, the baby is delivered dead. We think God judged Judah for burning children alive? May God have mercy on our souls because we have figured out a way to burn our children alive on the outside and the inside simultaneously. Israel did not repent, and God removed them from His sight. Judah did repent, and God still removed them from His sight. Israel and Judah had gone too far.

It is only American pride and arrogance that would cause us to think that God would not remove us from His sight for doing the very same things to Him as the nations of Israel and Judah. Romans 9–11 tell us that we were grafted into the tree (Israel). If God will remove the tree, what do you think He will do to the branches that were grafted into the tree? It is my prayer that we have not gone too far, and all that is left for us is judgment. On the Thomas Jefferson Memorial are inscribed these words of warning if we deviate from one nation under God: "Indeed, I tremble for my country when I reflect that God is just, that His justice cannot sleep forever."[4]

Appendix 1

Questions to Ask a Candidate

1. What does individual responsibility look like to you?

2. What is the most important aspect of family values?

3. Do you agree that family wealth should be left to the families, and how would you go about reducing inheritance taxes?

4. What evidence can you list for global warming, and how will you address this issue?

5. How would you go about reducing the national debt?

6. What solutions would you suggest for alien immigration?

7. Do you believe life begins at conception? How would you go about protecting the unborn?

8. How would you define marriage?

9. What ideas can you add to "the state has the right of capital punishment in cases of murder"?

10. How does "parents are responsible for raising their children" compare with your views on parental responsibility?

11. Why is presenting the message of Jesus Christ significant?

12. What solution would you suggest for keeping the right to bear arms in place?

13. What is the most important aspect of reducing racial tensions?

14. How does the United Nations support the United States' national sovereignty?

15. Do you agree that the United States should support the nation of Israel?

16. How is a strong military force related to national security, and what will you do to keep our military strong and on the cutting edge of defense?

17. Do you think those who work hard for what they have should redistribute it to those who do not work?

Notes

Introduction

1. William J. Federer, *Back Fired A Nation Born for Religious Tolerance No Longer Tolerate Religion*, (St. Louis, MO: Amerisearch, Inc., 2007), 19.

2. Edwin S. Gaustad, *Faith of Our Fathers* (San Francisco: Harper & Row, 1987), 161.

3. The Ryrie Study Bible, New American Standard Bible (Chicago: Moody Press, 1978), Matthew 28:18–20.

4. David Barton, *The Myth of Separation*, (Aledo, TX: Wallbuilders Press, 1991), 266.

5. Charles Finney, The independent, *The Decay of Conscientious*, (New York: December 4, 1873.

1 America's Past and Present, A Generational Change

1. Jack Hibbs, pastor of Calvary Chapel in Chino Hills, California

2. David Reagan, "The Decay of Society," *Lamplighter*, May/June 2012, 3.

3. Ibid.

4. Stephen K. McDowell and Mark A. Beliles, *America's Providential History* (Charlottesville, Virginia: Providence Press, 1988), 190.

5. Ibid.

6. Charles Finney, "The Decay of Conscientious," *The Independent*, (New York: December 4, 1873).

7. Ken Hamm and Brett Beemer with Todd Hillard, *Already Gone: Why Your Kids Will Quit Church and What You Can Do to Stop It* (Green Forest, AR: Master Books, 2009).

8. Peter Marshall and David Manuel, *The Light and the Glory* (Old Tappen, New Jersey: Fleming H. Revell Co., 1977), 370, Footnote 10.

9. M. E. Bradford, *A Worthy Company* (NH.: Plymouth Rock Foundation, 1982), X, All lists of delegates and their denominational affiliations are taken from the table of contents.

10. Steven C. Dawson, *God's Providence in American's History* (California: Steven C. Dawson, 1988), 9:6.

11. David Burton, *The Myth of Separation* (Aledo, Texas: Wallbuilders Press 1989).

12. David Burton, *The Myth of Separation* (Aledo, Texas: Wallbuilders Press 1989). *The New England Primer* (Boston, 1777).

13. David Burton, *America's Godly Heritage* (Aledo, Texas: Wallbuilders Press, 1992), video tape.

14. *The New England Primer* (Boston, 1777).

15. Russ Walton, *Biblical Principles of Importance to Godly Christians* (New Hampshire: Plymouth Rock Foundation, 1984), 353, 363.

16. Stephen K. McDowell and Mark A. Beliles, *America's Providential History* (Charlottesville, Virginia: Providence Press, 1988), 222.

17. W. D. Lewis, *Washington's Farewell Address and Webster's First Bunker Hill Oration* (New York: American Book Company, 1910), 23–24.

18. "Anti-Obama mail piece: We are no longer a Christian nation," last modified October 31, 2012, http://politicalticker.blogs.cnn.com/2012/10/31/anti-obama-mail-piece-we-are-no-longer-a-christian-nation/.

19. John Eidsmoe, *Christianity and the Constitution* (Michigan: Baker Book House, 1987), 52; David Burton, *America's Godly Heritage* (Aledo, Texas: Wallbuilders Press, 1992), video tape.

20. David Burton, *America's Godly Heritage* (Aledo, Texas: Wallbuilders Press, 1992), video tape. David Burton, *The Myth of Separation* (Aledo, Texas: Wallbuilders Press 1989), 56.

21. David Burton, *America's Godly Heritage* (Aledo, Texas: Wallbuilders Press, 1992), video tape; Stephen K. McDowell and Mark A. Beliles, *America's Providential History* (Charlottesville, Virginia: Providence Press, 1988), 144; Steven C. Dawson, *God's Providence in America's History* (Rancho Cordova, California: Steve C. Dawson, 1988).

22. The Ryrie Study Bible, New American Standard Bible (Chicago: Moody Press, 1978), Jeremiah 17. David Burton, America's Godly Heritage (Aledo, Texas: Wallbuilders Press, 1992), video tape.

23. David Burton, America's Godly Heritage (Aledo, Texas: Wallbuilders Press, 1992), video tape.

24. Ibid.

25. *Church of the Holy Trinity v. United States*; 143 U.S. 457 (1892).

26. Ibid.

27. *Vidal v. Girard's Executors*; 43 U.S. 127 (1844).

28. *People v. Ruggles*; 8 Johns 470 (1811).

29. The Constitution of the United States of America, First Amendment.

30. David Burton, *The Myth of Separation* (Aledo, Texas: Wallbuilders Press 1989), 46.

31. Edwin S. Gaustad, *Faith of Our Fathers* (San Francisco: Harper & Row, 1987), 157–158, cf. Gary DeMar, *God and Government: A Biblical and Historical Study* (Atlanta: American Vision Press, 1982), 171.

32. The Constitution of the United States of America, First Amendment.

33. David Burton, *The Myth of Separation* (Aledo, Texas: Wallbuilders Press 1989), Thomas Jefferson, January 1, 1802 in a personal letter to Nehemiah Dodge, Ephriam Robbins, and Stephen Nelson of the Dansbury Baptist Association, Danbury, Connecticut. *Reynolds v. U.S.*, 98 U.S. 164 (1878).

34. David Burton, *The Myth of Separation* (Aledo, Texas: Wallbuilders Press 1989), 132, 133.

35. Ibid.

36. *Reynolds v. U.S.*; 98 U.S. 164 (1878).

37. Ibid.

38. Ibid.

39. *Reynolds v. U.S.*; 98 U.S. 164 (1878). Stephen K. McDowell and Mark A. Beliles, *The Spirit of the Constitution* (Charlottesville, Virginia: Providence Press, 1988); David Burton, *The Myth of Separation* (Aledo, Texas: Wallbuilders Press 1989), 43.

40. *Everson v. Board of Education*; 330 U.S. 1 (1947).

41. David Burton, *The Myth of Separation* (Aledo, Texas: Wallbuilders Press 1989), 46.

42. *Baer v. Kolmorgen*; 181 N.Y.S. 2d, 230 (1958).

43. Gary Demar, *God and Government: A Biblical and Historical Study* (Atlanta: American Vision Press, 1982), 163.

44. Tim LaHaye, *Faith of Our Founding Fathers* (Brentwood, Tennessee: Wolgemuth & Hyatt, Publishers, Inc., 1987), 3.

45. *Abbington v. Schempp*; 374 U.S. 203 (1963).

46. Peter Marshall and David Manuel, *The Light and the Glory* (Old Tappen, New Jersey: Fleming H. Revell Co., 1977), 370, Footnote 10.

47. *Vidal v. Girard's Executors*; 43 U.S. 127 (1844).

48. *Engel v. Vitale*; 370 U.S. 421 (1962).

49. Ibid.

50. W. D. Lewis, Washington's *Farewell Address and Webster's First Bunker Hill Oration* (New York: American Book Company, 1910), 23–24.

51. *Stone v. Gramm*; 449 U.S. 39 (1980).

52. The Ryrie Study Bible, New American Standard Bible (Chicago: Moody Press, 1978), Exodus 20:1–17.

53. *Time*, February 1, 1988

54. Russ Walton, *Biblical Principles of Importance to Godly Christians* (New Hampshire: Plymouth Rock Foundation, 1984), 361, cf. Stephen K. McDowell and Mark A. Beliles, "Principles for the Reformation of a Nation" (Charlottesville, Virginia: Providence Press, 1988), 54.

55. Steven C. Dawson, *God's Providence in America's History* (Rancho Cordova, California: Steve C. Dawson, 1988), 54.

56. The Ryrie Study Bible, New American Standard Bible (Chicago: Moody Press, 1978), Matthew 5:21–22.

57. Ibid., Matthew 5:27–28.

58. Pat Robertson, *America's Dates With Destiny* (Nashville: Thomas Nelson Publishers, 1986), 93, 94. Quoted from John Adams, in *The Works of John Adams*, Second President of the United States

collected by Charles Francis Adams (Boston: Little, Brown, 1854).

59. Abraham Lincoln. 1863, in a reply to a remark that "The Lord was on the Union's side." Frank B. Carpenter, Six Months at the White House (1866), 125. J. B. McClure, ed., *Abraham Lincoln's Stories and Speeches* (Chicago: Rhodes & McClure Pub. Co., 1896), 185–186. John Wesley Hill, *Abraham Lincoln: Man of God* (NY: G.P. Putnam & Sons, 1920), 330.

60. The Ryrie Study Bible, New American Standard Bible (Chicago: Moody Press, 1978), Deuteronomy 25:3.

61. John Eidsmoe, *Christianity and the Constitution* (Michigan Baker Book House, 1987), 325.

62. Charles Finney, "The Decay of Conscientious," *The Independent*, (New York: December 4, 1873).

63. The Ryrie Study Bible, New American Standard Bible (Chicago: Moody Press, 1978), 2 Timothy 3:1–5.

64. Ibid., John 8:32.

2 God's Word Is the Standard of Truth

1. The Ryrie Study Bible, New American Standard Bible (Chicago: Moody Press, 1978), 2 John 10 & 3 John 5–8.

2. Ibid., Matthew 10:40–42.

3. Ibid., 1 Kings 13:18–24.

4. Ibid., Matthew 16:13–17.

5. Ibid., Matthew 16:18–20.

6. Ibid., Matthew 16:21–23.

7. Ibid., John 17:1–3.

8. Tim LaHaye, *Faith of Our Founding Fathers* (Brentwood, Tennessee: Wolgemuth & Hyatt, Publishers, Inc., 1987), 123, 124. Quoted from *The Debates in the Federal Convention of 1787 Which Framed the Constitution of the United States of America*, reported by James Madison (New York: Oxford University Press, 1920), 181, 182. Stephen K. McDowell and Mark A. Beliles, *America's Providential History* (Charlottesville, Virginia: Providence Press, 1988), 7, 142. David Burton, *America's Godly Heritage* (Aledo, Texas: Wallbuilders Press, 1992), video tape.

3 Christians Are to Vote on Economic Issues

1. The Ryrie Study Bible, New American Standard Bible (Chicago: Moody Press, 1978), 1 John 3:13–18.

2. Ibid., Genesis 2:21–25.

3. Ibid., Mark 14:3–9.

4. Alexis de Tocqueville, *Democracy in America*. 2 vols. 1840. New York: Vintage Books, 1945. 1:315.

5. John Locke, "Second Essay Concerning Civil Government." *Great Books of the Western World*, vol. 35. (Chicago: Encyclopedia Britannica, Inc., 1952). 36, par. 52.

6. Ibid., 37, par. 58.

7. Ibid., 37, par. 59.

8. The Ryrie Study Bible, New American Standard Bible (Chicago: Moody Press, 1978), Ephesians 5:22–6:4.

9. William F. Jasper, "Cooking Climate Consensus Data: '97% of Scientists Affirm Agw' Debunked," *The New American*, June 25, 2013, http://www.thenewamerican.com/tech/environment/item/15624–cooking-climate-consensus-data05 June 2013–97–of-scientists-affirm-agw-debunked.

10. Ibid.

11. "Global Warming Hoax—Leading Scientists Debunk Climate Alarmism," February 27, 2012. http://poleshift.ning.com/profiles/blogs/global-warming-hoax-leading-scientists-debunk-climate-alarmism.

12. The Ryrie Study Bible, New American Standard Bible (Chicago: Moody Press, 1978), Ecclesiastes 5:18–19.

13. Ibid., 1 Timothy 6:6–10.

14. Ibid., Hebrews 13:5–6.

15. Thomas Jefferson, *The Writings of Thomas Jefferson*. Edited by Paul Leicester Ford. 10 vols. New York: G.P. Putnam & Sons, 1892–99. 4:414.

16. Thomas Jefferson, *The Writings of Thomas Jefferson*. Edited by Albert Ellery Bergh. 20 vols. Washington: The Thomas Jefferson memorial Association, 1907. 13:357–58.

17. The Ryrie Study Bible, New American Standard Bible (Chicago: Moody Press, 1978), Genesis 45:16–18.

18. Ibid., Exodus 12:49; Leviticus 24:22; Numbers 15:15–16.

19. Ibid., 2 Chronicles 30:23–27.

20. Ibid., Deuteronomy 17:18–20.

21. Ibid., Jeremiah 22:1–5.

22. http://www.fairus.org/site/PageServer? pagename=iic_immigrationissuecenters7fd8.

23. http://www.cis.org/articles/2004/fiscalexec.HTML

24. http://www.cis.org/articles/2004/fiscalexec.HTML

25. http://transcripts.cnn.com/TRANscriptS/ 0604/01/ldt…0.HTML

26. http://transcripts.cnn.com/TRANscriptS/ 0604/01/ldt.01.HTML

27. http://transcripts.CNN.com/%20TRANscriptS/ 0604/01/ldt.01.HTML<http://transcripts.CNN. com/%20TRANscriptS/0604/01/ldt.01.HTML>

28. HTTPS://owa.slugger.com/owa/UrlBlockedError. aspx

29. http://premium.cnn.com/TRANSCIPTS/ 0610/29/ldt.01.HTML

30. http://transcripts.cnn.com/TRANSCRI

31. http:// www.drdsk.com/articleshtml

4 Christians Are to Vote on Social Issues

1. The Ryrie Study Bible, New American Standard Bible (Chicago: Moody Press, 1978), Luke 1:39–44.

2. Ibid., Exodus 21:22–24.

3. Ibid., Genesis 2:18–25.

4. Ibid., Genesis 1:26–28.

5. Ibid., Romans 1:26–27.

6. Ibid., Romans 1:29–32.

7. The Williams Institute, UCLA Study, 2011. http://en.wikipedia.org/wiki/LGBT_demographics_of_the_United_States.

8. The Ryrie Study Bible, New American Standard Bible (Chicago: Moody Press, 1978), Deuteronomy 6:6–7, Proverbs 22:6; & Ephesians 6:4.

9. Ibid., Mark 16:15; Matthew 28:18–20.

10. Ibid., Colossians 2:9–15.

11. Ibid., Luke 9:3–5; Matthew 10:7–10.

12. The Constitution of the United States of America, Second Amendment.

13. The Ryrie Study Bible, New American Standard Bible (Chicago: Moody Press, 1978), Galatians 2:11–14.

5 Christians Are to Vote
on Foreign Affairs Issues

1. The Ryrie Study Bible, New American Standard Bible (Chicago: Moody Press, 1978), Jeremiah 18:7–10.

2. Ibid., Daniel 2:19–23.

3. Margaret Clarkson, *Destined for Glory: The Meaning of Suffering* (Grand Rapids: Eerdmans, 1963), 75.

4. The Ryrie Study Bible, New American Standard Bible (Chicago: Moody Press, 1978), Deuteronomy 28:64–67.

5. Ibid., Isaiah 11:6–9.

6. Ibid., Isaiah 35:1–7.

7. Ibid., Joel 2:21–26.

8. Ibid., Zechariah 12:6.

9. Ibid., Zechariah 12:10.

10. Ibid., Deuteronomy 30:1–9.

11. Ibid., Ezekiel 36:22–30.

12. Ibid., 1 Thessalonians 4:13–18.

13. Ibid., Zechariah 14:1–9.

14. Ibid., Revelation 19:17–21.

15. Ibid., Revelation 20:1–6.

16. Ibid., Isaiah 11:6–9.

17. Ibid., Micah 4:1–7.

18. Ibid., Revelation 20:7–10.

19. George Washington. *The Writings of George Washington*, Edited by John C. Fitzpatrick. 39 vols. Washington: United States Government Printing Office, 1931–44. 33:165.

20. Ibid.

21. William V. Wells. The Life and Public Services of Samuel Adams. 3 vols. Boston: Little, Brown and Company, 1865. 1:504.

22. Benjamin Franklin. *The Writings of Benjamin Franklin*. Edited by Albert Henry Smyth. 10 vols. New York: The Macmillan Company, 1905–7. 2:352.

23. Ibid., 6:3–4.

24. Nicholas Wade. *A World Beyond Healing: The Prologue and Aftermath of Nuclear War*, W. W. Norton and Company. 1987.

25. Jonathan Schell, *The Fate of the Earth*, Mass Market paperback. 1982.

26. The Ryrie Study Bible, New American Standard Bible (Chicago: Moody Press, 1978), Matthew 35:19–30.

27. Ibid., 1 Thessalonians 4:13–18.

28. Ibid., Philippians 3:20–21.

29. Ibid., Romans 8:29–30.

30. Ibid., Matthew 5:4–12.

31. Ibid., 2 Timothy 2:16–18.

32. Ibid., 1 Corinthians 9:24–27.

33. Ibid., 1 Peter 5:1–4.

6 The Answers to Our Problems Is Found in God's Word

1. The Ryrie Study Bible, New American Standard Bible (Chicago: Moody Press, 1978), Jonah 3:5–9.

2. David Barton, *The Myth of Separation*, (Aledo, TX: Wallbuilders Press, 1991), 266.

3. The Ryrie Study Bible, New American Standard Bible (Chicago: Moody Press, 1978), 2 Kings 23:26–27.

4. Thomas Jefferson. Jefferson Memorial, Washington, DC.